iPhon

The Newest Amazing Tips & Tricks Guide for iPhone X, XR, XS, and XS Max Users

(The User Manual like No Other (Tips & Tricks Edition))

Phila Perry

ISBN: 978-1-63750-245-7

Table of Contents

Introduction

Here comes the newest amazing tips and tricks guide for all iPhone X, XR, XS, and XS Max Users (regularly updated).

There are tips that you would not find in the official Apple resources, which we have put together in this comprehensive book for all iPhone users, especially for you, we have collected in this book the most common tips of the new iPhone X series.

This is the complete guide for you, as you would get simplified follow-through instructions on every possible thing you should know about iPhone X, XR, XS & XS Max, how you can customize the iPhone as well as amazing Tips & tricks you never would find in the original iPhone manual.

If you have not purchased it yet, and want to try iPhone X, you have nothing to worry about, because this book has a lot of information, tips and tricks for the perfect mobile phone that would improve your user experience and life. The whole process is as fast as you can imagine. Only a few steps will require some technical approach and workarounds that would turn you into an iPhone geek and guru in no time.

This Tips and Tricks guide would also get you equipped with basic knowledge on how to take the maximum advantage of your *iCloud*, *how to troubleshoot & fix some iPhone problems yourself without stress, advanced tips and tricks that will make you a Pro in less than 30minutes of reading this book,* and lot more.

Also, this book is simple enough to understand and a

follow-through ***Tips & Tricks Guide*** *suitable for kids, adolescents, teens, and adults*, even for beginners or dummies, seniors, or an expert in the computer and technology niche.

Phila Perry's book helps you accomplish everything you would need to know and learn in a more simplified and enjoyable form.

After reading this, you can use your phone to the fullest.

Chapter 1

How to Set up Your brand-new iPhone XR the correct way

For many individuals, the iPhone XR would be radically not the same as previous iPhones. Not surprisingly, the iPhone set up process hasn't transformed much. However, you might end up on the familiar ground; you may still find a lot of little things you honestly must do before you turn up your new phone for the very first time (or soon after that).

Let's check out how to set up your brand-new iPhone XR the proper way.

Setup iPhone XR the Correct Way

With iPhone XR, you'll have the ability to take benefit of

Apple's Automatic Setup. If you're through a mature iPhone without Face Identification, you would see that Touch ID is entirely gone. (Which means you'll save one face, rather than several.)

If you're a serial upgrader, and you're from the year-old iPhone X, less has changed. But you'll still need to update just as usual.

Restoring from a back-up of Your old iPhone

It's probably that you'll be restoring your brand-new iPhone from a back-up of your present iPhone. If that's so, then you merely want to do a couple of things:

- Be sure you come with an up-to-date backup.
- Use Apple's new Auto Setup feature to get you

started truly.

The first thing is as simple as going to the iCloud configurations on your iPhone, and looking at that, there surely is a recent automated back-up. If not, do one by hand. Head to *Configurations > Your Name > iCloud > iCloud Back-up and tap* ***BACKUP Now***. Wait around until it is done.

Auto Setup for iPhone XR

Secondly; Auto Setup enables you to duplicate your Apple ID and home Wi-Fi configurations from another device, simply by getting them close collectively.

In case your old iPhone (or iPad) has already been operating iOS 11 or iOS 12, to put it simply the devices next to one another. Then follow the prompts to avoid needing to enter your Apple ID and Wi-Fi passwords; this makes the original iPhone set up much smoother.

Set up a fresh iPhone XR from Scratch

The guide below assumes you're establishing your brand-new iPhone from scratch. If you don't wish to accomplish that, you'll need to acquire any of the other iPhone manual for begginers that I have written.

iPhone XR Set up: The Fundamentals

Re-download only the applications you will need - That one is crucial. Most of us have so many applications on our iPhones that people do not use; this is the big reason we execute a clean set up, in all honesty. Utilize the App Store application and make sure you're authorized into the Apple accounts. (Touch the tiny icon of the Updates - panel to see which accounts you're logged on to.) Only download applications you've found in the past half a year. Or, be daring: download stuff you utilize regularly. We're prepared to wager it'll be considered a very few.

Set up ***DO NOT Disturb*** - If you're like ordinary people, you're constantly getting notifications, iMessages, and other types of distractions through to your iPhone. Create ***DO NOT Disturb*** in the Configurations application (it's in the next section listed below, slightly below *Notifications* and *Control Center*). You'll want to routine it for occasions when you need never to be bothered.

Toggle Alarm to On and then Messages when you want to keep Notifications away from that person. Try 9 p.m. to 8 a.m. when you can.

Pro suggestion: Let some things through if there's an

Emergency: Enable Allow Phone calls From your Favorites and toggle Repeated Phone calls to On. iOS 12 also enables you to switch on *DO NOT Disturb* at Bedtime, which mutes all notifications and even hides them from the lock screen, and that means you don't get distracted when you take the phone to check time.

Set up Face ID

Face ID is much simpler to use than Touch ID, and it's own also simpler to create. Instead of needing to teach your iPhone with your fingerprints, one at a time, you simply check out the camera, and that's almost it. To create Face ID on your iPhone, do the next when prompted through the preliminary iPhone setup. (If you'd like to begin over with a phone you set up previously, check out *Settings > Face ID & Passcode, and type in your password, to begin.*)

Establishing Face ID is similar to the compass calibration your iPhone enables you to do from time to time when you use the Maps app. Only rather than rolling the iPhone around, you roll your head. You'll need to do two scans, and then the iPhone XR will have your 3D head stored in its Secure Enclave, inaccessible to anything - even to iOS itself (despite some clickbait "news" stories).

Now, still in *Configurations > Face ID & Passcode*, you can pick which features to use with Face ID, like everyone else did with *Touch ID*.

If you regularly sport another appearance - you're a clown, a doctor, an Elvis impersonator, or something similar - then additionally, you should create another appearance. Just tap the button in the facial ID settings to set this up.

Create iPhone Email

- ***Add your email accounts*** - Whether you utilize Mail, Perspective, or something similar to Sparrow, you'll want to include your email accounts immediately. For Apple's Email app, touch *Configurations > Accounts & Passwords, then touch Add Accounts*. Choose your email supplier and follow the steps to enter all the knowledge required.

- ***See more email preview*** - Email lets you start to see the content of a note without starting it. May as well see as a lot of it as you possibly can, right? Utilize Settings > Email and tap on the Preview button. Change your configurations to five lines and get more information from your email messages and never have to get them open up.

- ***Established your default accounts*** - For reasons unknown, our iOS Email settings always appear to default to a merchant account we never use, like ***iCloud***. Tap *Configurations > Accounts & Passwords > Your email accounts name, and then touch Accounts > Email*. Once you reach the depths of the settings, you can touch your preferred email; this will be utilized as your address in new mails. (When there is only one address in here, you're all set.) That is also the spot to add some other email addresses associated with your email account.

Advanced iPhone email tweaks

- ***Swipe to control email*** - It's much more helpful to

have the ability to swipe your email messages away rather than clicking through and tapping on several control keys. Swipe to Archive, so that whenever you swipe that path, you'll have the ability to either quickly save a contact to your Archive. Or, if your email accounts support swiping left as a default Delete action, it'll offer a Garbage icon. Swipe left to Tag as Read, which is a smart way to slam through your electronic mails as you have them. This only impacts your built-in Email application from Apple. Each third-party email customer can do things differently.

- ***Add an HTML signature*** - A good email signature really can cause you to look professional, so make sure to include an HTML signature to your email. If you've already got one on the desktop, duplicate and paste the code into contact and ahead to yourself. You'll be able to duplicate and paste it into an Email application (or whichever email supplier you like, if it facilitates it). It could be as easy as textual content formatting tags or as complicated as adding a logo design from a webserver. You should use an iOS application to make one, too; however they tend to look fairly basic or clip-art-y.

Manage Calendars, iCloud, Communications and more

- ***Set default Calendar alert times*** - Calendar is ideal for alerting you to important occasions, but it's not necessarily at a convenient or useful time.

Established the default timing on three types of occasions: Birthdays, Occasions, and All-Day Occasions, and that means you get reminders when they're helpful. Utilize *Configurations > Calendars*. Tap on Default Alert Times and set your Birthday reminders to 1 day before, your Occasions to quarter-hour before (or a period which makes more sense to your mind), and All-Day Occasions on the day of the function (10 a.m.). You'll never miss a meeting again.

- ***Background application refresh*** - You'll desire to be selective about which applications you desire to be in a position to run in the backdrop, so have a look at the list in *Settings > General > Background App Refresh.* Toggle Background App Refresh to ON, then toggle OFF all the applications you don't need being able to access anything in the background. When in question, toggle it to OFF and find out if you are slowed up by any applications that require to refresh when you release them. You'll want to allow Background Refresh for Cult of Macintosh Magazine!

iCloud Everywhere

- ***iCloud is everything*** - There's without a doubt in our thoughts that iCloud is the easiest, optimum solution for keeping all of your stuff supported and safe. Utilize the Configurations > iCloud and be sure to register with your **Apple ID**. You can manage your storage space in here, but make sure to enable all you need immediatel. Enable iCloud Drive, Photos, Connections, Reminders, Safari, Records, News, Wallet, Back-up, Kechain and others once you get the iPhone unpacked. You can enable Email and Calendars if you merely use Apple's applications and services; normally, you will keep those toggled to OFF.

More iPhone set up Tweaks

- ***Extend your Auto-Lock*** - Let's face it. The default two minutes you get for the Volume of time your iPhone will remain on without turning off its screen may keep the battery higher much longer, but it's insufficient for anybody during normal use. Utilize Configurations, General, Auto-Lock to create this to the utmost five minutes which means you can stop tapping your screen at all times to keep it awake.

- ***Get texts everywhere*** - You can enable your Mac PC or iPad to get texts from your iPhone, provided you've set up iMessage to them (Settings, Text messages, toggle iMessage to ON on any iOS device, Messages Preferences on your Mac). Ensure that your other device is close by when you utilize Settings on your iPhone, then touch Messages > TEXT Forwarding. Any devices available will arrive on the list. Toggle your Mac or iPad to On, and then check the prospective device for a code. Enter that code into your iPhone. Now all of your devices are certain to get not only iMessages but also texts from those not using iMessage.

- ***Equalize your tunes*** - Start the EQ in your Music application to be able to hear your preferred jams and never have a trouble with a bluetooth speaker. Go to Configurations > Music. Once there, touch on EQ and established your iPhone to NIGHT TIME; this will provide you with a great quantity raise for those times where you want to blast *The Clash* while you make a quick supper in the kitchen.

Secure Your Web Experience

- ***Safari set up*** - Surfing the net is filled with forms to complete. Adding your name, address, email, and bank cards may take up a great deal of your power. Make sure to head into Configurations > Safari > AutoFill to create your mobile internet browser the proper way. First, toggle Use Contact Info to On. Then tap on My Info and select the contact you want to use when you encounter form areas in Safari. Toggle Titles and Passwords on as well, and that means you can save that across appointments to the same website. (This pulls from iCloud Keychain, so make sure to have that allowed, too.)

Toggle CREDIT CARDS to On as well, which means you can shop swiftly. (be sure to only use SSL-encrypted websites.)

Pro suggestion: Manage which bank cards your iPhone helps you to save with a tap on BANK CARDS. You can include new cards within, or delete ones that no more work or that you don't want to use via mobile Safari.

Safari in iOS 12 and later version also blocks cross-site

monitoring, which are those cookies that follow you around and let online stores place the same advertisements on every subsequent web page you visit. That is On by default, and that means you should not do anything. Just relax and revel in your newfound personal privacy.

Services subscription during iPhone setup

- ***Enable iCloud Photo Library*** - We love the iCloud Photo Library. It maintains your photos and videos securely stored in the cloud and enable you to get full-quality copies of your documents in the event you misplace your originals. iCloud Picture Library depends on your iCloud storage space, if you have a lot of photos, you'll want to bump that up. Utilize Configurations > iCloud > Photos, then toggle iCloud Image Library to On. (Remember that this will switch off My Picture Stream. If you'd like both, you'll need to re-toggle Image Stream back again to On.)

- ***Use iTunes Match*** - Sure, Apple Music monitors all the music data files on your devices, but if you delete them from your iPhone and don't have a back-up elsewhere, you're heading to have to stay for whatever quality Apple Music will provide you with when you listen. If you wish to maintain your full-resolution music documents supported to the cloud, use iTunes Match. You get all of your music files matched up or published to iCloud in the best bitrate possible. After that you can stream or download the music to any device provided your iTunes Match membership is intact. Never be without your music (or have an over-filled iPhone) again. Go to *Configurations* > *Music*. Then touch on Sign up to iTunes Match to understand this valuable service allowed on your brand-new iPhone.

Chapter 2

iPhone X: All You Need to Know!

Apple introduced iPhone X (X pronounced "10") at the other dressing up event at Steve Careers Theater in the Apple Recreation area on Sept 12, alongside iPhone 8 and iPhone 8 Plus. It's was high quality, high-end model in Apple's 2017 iPhone lineup, before iPhone 11 and iPhone 11 pro came.

It features an all-screen design, a 5.8-inch OLED screen, cellular charging, dual-lens cameras with improved depth sensing, and a cosmetic recognition system called Face ID, and lacks the iconic Home button.

iPhone X Hardware Specifications

Apple's flagship iPhone includes a 5.8-inch diagonal

OLED screen with 2436-by-1125-pixel resolution at 458 ppi dubbed Very Retina HD. The screen features True Firmness technology that was first launched in iPad Pro in 2016. It uses ambient light detectors to adjust the screen's white balance to the encompassing ambient light. It will come in two storage space capacities: 64GB and 256GB, and will come in two color options: space grey and silver.

It is powered by Apple's new A11 Bionic chip with 64-little bit structures. The A11 Bionic system-on-chip carries a Hexa-core processor chip with two cores optimized for performance that is 25% faster than the A10 Fusion processor chip, and four efficiency-optimised cores that are 70% faster than the prior era. The A11 Bionic chip also features the first Apple-designed images processing device and a Neural Engine. The Neural

Engine is purpose-built for machine learning, a kind of artificial cleverness that enables computer systems to study from observation. It is utilized for realizing people, places, and items, and iPhone X's new features like Face ID and Animoji.

In addition, it features Face ID, a face acknowledgement system, which replaces Touch ID, Apple's fingerprint sensor. THE FACIAL ID sensor includes two modules: a dot projector internally called the *"Romeo"* tasks more than 30,000 infrared dots onto the user's face, and the infrared camera internally called *"Juliet"* reads the design. The pattern is then delivered to the Secure Enclave in the A11 Bionic chip to verify a match with the phone owner's face. Face ID has received reviews that are positive from users and critics. However, it's been popular and miss with similar twins and has been misled by a particular 3D printed face mask.

It includes a dual-camera system at the back. The dual-cameras are positioned vertically, unlike iPhone 7 Plus. The 12-megapixel wide-angle camera has an f/1.8 aperture that helps face detection, high active range, and optical image stabilization. The supplementary, telephoto zoom lens features 2× optical centre and 10× digital move with a wider aperture of f/2.4. In addition, it features optical image stabilization, which wasn't available on iPhone 7 Plus. It gives you to consider photos with specific depth-of-field using the Family portrait mode. You can even take photos with Lightning results in portrait setting because of the dual-sensing video cameras and cosmetic mapping. In addition, it has a quad-LED True Shade adobe flash with 2× better light uniformity. iPhone X is with the capacity of taking 4K video at 24, 30 or 60 fps, or 1080p video at 30, 60, 120, or 240 fps.

iPhone X's rear-camera earned 97 factors from DxOMark, a respected source of indie image quality measurements and rankings for smartphone, camera, and zoom lens, just behind the Google Pixel 2 with 98 factors.

The front-facing camera includes a 7-megapixel TrueDepth camera with f/2.2 aperture, and features face recognition and HDR. It is capable of recording 1080p video at 30 fps, or 720p video at 240 fps. It also works with a great new feature called *Animoji* that is exclusively on the iPhone X. The front-facing TrueDepth camera catches and analyzes more than 50 different muscle motions, and then mirrors your expressions in virtually any of 12 different Animoji. Some creative iPhone X users have used the feature to produce lip-sync videos dubbed Animoji Karaoke, that was one of the trending topics on Twitter when it premiered

Chapter 3

How to Customize Your iPhone

Customize iPhone Home Screen

You may take a look at your iPhone home screen more than some other single screen so that it should be set up the way you want it to appear. Below are a few options for customizing your iPhone home screen.

- ***Change Your Wallpaper***: You may make the image behind your applications on the home screen just about whatever you want. A favourite picture of your children or spouse or the logo design of your preferred team are a few options. Find the wallpaper settings by heading to *Settings -> Wallpaper -> Select a New Wallpaper*.

- ***Use Live or Video Wallpaper***: Want something eye-catching? Use cartoon wallpapers instead. There are a few restrictions, but this is fairly cool. *Head to Settings -> Wallpaper -> Select a New Wallpaper -> pick and choose Active or Live.*

- ***Put Apps into Folders***: Organize your home screen centred on how you utilize applications by grouping them into folders. Begin by gently tapping and securing one application until all your apps begin to tremble. Then pull and drop one application onto another to place those two applications into a folder.

- ***Add Extra Webpages of Apps***: All your apps won't need to be about the same home screen. You may make individual "webpages" for different kinds of applications or different users by tapping and keeping applications or folders, then dragging them from the right side of the screen. Browse the *"Creating Web pages on iPhone"* portion of How to Manage Apps on the iPhone Home Screen to get more.

Customize iPhone Lock Screen

Like everyone else, you can customize your home screen, you can customize the iPhone lock screen, too. In this manner, you have control over the very first thing you see each time you wake up your phone.

- ***Customize Lock Screen Wallpaper***: Exactly like on the home screen, you can transform your iPhone lock screen wallpaper to employ a picture, computer animation, or video. Browse the link within the last section for details.

- ***Create a Stronger Passcode***: The much longer your passcode, the harder it is to break right into your iPhone (you are utilizing a passcode, right?). The default passcode is 4 or 6 character types (depending on your iOS version); nevertheless, you make it much longer and stronger. *Head to Settings -> Face ID (or Touch ID) & Passcode -> Change Passcode and following an instructions.*

- ***Get Suggestions from Siri***: Siri can learn your practices, preferences, passions, and location and then use that information to suggest content for you. Control what Siri suggests by heading to *Configurations -> Siri & Search -> Siri Recommendations and setting the things you want to use to On/green.*

Customize iPhone Ringtones & Text message Tones

The ringtones and text tones your iPhone uses to get your attention need not be exactly like everyone else's. You may make all types of changes, including changing tone, and that means you know who's phoning or texting without even taking a glance at your phone.

- ***Change the Default Ringtone***: Your iPhone comes pre-loaded with a large number of ringtones. Change the default ringtone for all those calls to the main one you prefer the better to get notified when you experience a call to arrive. Do this by *heading to Settings -> Noises (Noises & Haptics on some models) -> Ringtone.*

- ***Set Person Ringtones***: You can assign a different ringtone for everybody in your connections list. That way, a love track can play whenever your partner calls, and you know it's them before even looking. Do that by heading to *Phone -> Connections -> tapping the individual whose ringtone you want to improve -> Edit -> Ringtone*.

- ***Get Full-Screen Photos for Incoming Phone calls***: The incoming call screen does not have to be boring. With this suggestion, you can view a fullscreen picture of the individual calling you. Go to *Mobile phone -> Connections -> touch the individual -> Edit -> Add Picture.*

- ***Customize Text Tone***: Like everyone else can customize the ringtones that play for calls, you can customize the appearance like video when you get texts. Go to *Configurations -> Seems (Noises & Haptics on some models) -> Text message Tone.*

TIPS: You're not limited by the band and text tone that include the iPhone. You can purchase ringtones from Apple, and some applications help you create your tone.

Customize iPhone Notifications

Your iPhone helpfully notifies you to understand when you have calls, text messages, emails, and other bits of information that may interest you. But those notifications can be irritating. Customize how you get notifications with these pointers.

- ***Choose Your Notification Style***: The iPhone enables you to choose lots of notification styles, from simple pop-ups to a mixture of sound and text messages, and more. Find the notification options in *Settings -> Notifications -> touch the application you want to regulate -> choose Alerts, Banner Style, Noises, and more.*

- ***Group Notifications from the Same App***: Get yourself a great deal of notifications from an individual app, but won't need to see each one taking space on your screen? You can group notifications into a *"stack"* that occupies the same space as your notification. Control this on the per-app basis by heading to *Settings -> Notifications -> the application you want to regulate -> Notification Grouping.*

- ***Adobe flashes a Light for Notifications***: Unless you want to try out to get a notification, you may make the camera adobe flashlight instead. It's a delicate, but apparent, option for most situations. Set this up in *Settings -> General -> Convenience -> Hearing -> move the LED Screen for Notifications slider to On/green.*

- ***Get Notification Previews with Face ID***: In case your iPhone has Face ID, you can utilize it to keep the notifications private. This establishing shows a simple headline in notifications; however, when you go through the screen and get identified by Face ID, the notification expands showing more content. Establish this by going to *Settings -> Notifications -> Show Previews -> When Unlocked.*

TIPS: That link also offers an awesome tip about using Face ID to silent alarms and notification sounds i.e

"Reduce Alarm Volume and Keep Screen Shiny with Attention Awareness."

- ***Get more information with Notification Center Widgets***: Notification Center not only gathers all your notifications, but it also offers up widgets, mini-versions of applications to enable you to do things without starting apps whatsoever.

iPhone Customizations that makes things Better to see

It isn't always readable text message or onscreen items on your iPhone, but these customizations make things much simpler to see.

- ***Use Screen Focus***: Do all the onscreen symbols and text message look a little too small for your eye? Screen Move magnifies your iPhone screen automatically. To utilize this option, go to *Settings -> Screen & Brightness -> View -> Zoomed -> Collection.*

TIP: *Most iPhone model support Screen Zoom, however the iPhone XS will not (although XS Max will).*

- ***Change Font Size***: The default font size on your iPhone may be a little small for your eye; nevertheless, you can raise it to make reading convenient. Head to *Settings -> General -> Availability -> Larger Text message -> move the slider to On/green -> change the slider below.*

- ***Use Dark mode***: If the shiny colours of the iPhone screen strain your eye, you may choose to use Dark Setting, which inverts shiny colors to darker ones. Find the essential Dark settings in *Configurations -> General -> Convenience -> Screen Accommodations -> Invert Colors*.

Other iPhone Customization Options

Here's an assortment of a few of our other favourite ways to customize our iPhones.

- ***Delete Pre-Installed Apps***: Got a couple of applications pre-installed on your iPhone you don't use? You can delete them (well, the majority of them, anyhow)! Just use the typical way to delete apps: Touch and keep until they tremble, then tap the x on the application icon.

- ***Customize Control Center***: Control Center has a lot more options than are apparent initially.

Customize Control Center to get just the group of tools you want to use. Head to *Settings -> Control Center -> Customize Settings.*

- ***Install your prefered Keyboard***: The iPhone includes a very good onscreen keypad; nevertheless, you can install third-party keyboards that add cool features, like *Google search, emojis, and GIFs, plus much more.* Get yourself a new keyboard at the App Store, then go to *Settings -> General -> Keyboard -> Keyboards.*

- ***Make Siri a friend***: Choose to have Siri talk with you utilizing a man's tone of voice? It could happen. Head to *Settings -> Siri & Search -> Siri Tone of voice -> Male*. You can even go with different accents if you want.

- ***Change Safari's default search engine***: Have search engines apart from Google that you'd like to use? Make it the default for those queries in Safari. Head to *Settings -> Safari -> Search Engine and making a fresh selection.*

- ***Make Your Shortcuts***: If you an iPhone X or newer version user, you can create all sorts of cool customized gestures and shortcuts for various jobs.

- ***Jailbreak Your Phone***: To obtain the most control over customizing your mobile phone, you can jailbreak it; this gets rid of Apple's settings over certain types of customization. Jailbreaking can cause specialized problems and lessen your phone's security, but it can give more control.

Chapter 4

iPhone XR Gestures You Should Know

Just like the iPhone X launched in 2017, the iPhone XR doesn't include a physical home button, instead deciding on gestures to regulate the new user interface. It will require a couple of days to get used to the change but stay with it. By day three, you'll question how you ever coped without it, and using an "old" iPhone will appear old and antiquated.

1. **Unlock your iPhone XR:** Go through the phone and swipe up from underneath the screen. It truly is that easy, and also you don't need to hold back for the padlock icon at the very top to improve to the unlock visual before swiping up.

2. **Touch to wake:** Tap on your iPhone XR screen

when it's off to wake it up and find out what notifications you have. To unlock it with FaceID, you'll still have to set it up.

3. **Back to the Homescreen:** Whatever application you are in if you would like to return to the Home screen, swipe up from underneath of the screen. If you're within an application that is operating scenery, you'll need to keep in mind slipping up from underneath the screen (i.e., the medial side) rather than where, in fact, the Home button used to be.

4. **Have a screenshot:** Press the power button and the volume up button together quickly, and it will snap a screenshot of whatever is on the screen.

5. **Addressing Control Centre:** It used to be always a swipe up, now it's a swipe down from the very

best right of the screen. Even though iPhone XR doesn't have 3D Touch, you can still long-press on the symbols to gain usage of further configurations within each icon.

6. **Accessing open up apps:** Previously you raise tapped on the home button to uncover what apps you'd open. You now swipe up and then pause with your finger on the screen. After that, you can see the applications you have opened up in the order you opened them.

7. **Launch Siri:** When you may use the "Hey Siri" hot term to awaken Apple's digital associate, there are still ways to release the function utilizing a button press. Press and contain the wake/rest button on the right aspect of the phone before Siri interface arises on screen.

8. **<u>Switch your phone off</u>:** Because long-pressing the wake/rest button launches Siri now, there's a fresh way for switching the phone off. To take action, you will need to press and contain the wake/rest button and the volume down button at the same time. Now glide to power off.

9. **<u>Release Apple Pay</u>:** Again, the wake/rest button is the main element here. Double touch it, and it will talk about your Apple Budget, then scan that person, and it'll request you to keep your phone near to the payment machine.

10. **<u>Gain access to widgets on the lock screen</u>:** Swipe from still left to directly on your lock screen, ideal for checking your activity bands.

Using Memoji

- **<u>Create your Memoji</u>:** Open up Messages and begin a new meaning. Touch the tiny monkey icon above the keypad, and then strike the "+" button to generate your personality. You will customize face form, skin tone, curly hair colour, eye, jewellery, plus much more.

- **<u>Use your Memoji/Animoji in a FaceTime call</u>:** Take up a FaceTime call, then press the tiny star icon underneath the corner. Now, tap the Memoji you want to use.

- **<u>Memoji your selfies</u>:** So, if you select your Memoji face preferably to your true to life face, you can send selfies with the Memoji changing your head in Messages. Take up a new message and touch the camera icon, and then press that top button. Now choose the Animoji option by tapping that monkey's mind again. Choose your Memoji and tap the 'x,' not the "done" button, and then take your picture.

- **Record a Memoji video:** Sadly, Memoji isn't available as a choice in the camera app, but that doesn't mean you can't record one. Much like the picture selfie, go to communications, touch on the camera icon and then slip to video and then tap on the superstar. Weight the Animoji or your Memoji, and off you decide to go.

iOS 12 iPhone XR Notification Tips

- ***Notifications collection to provide quietly***: If you're worried that you will be getting way too many notifications, you can place the way they deliver with an app by application basis. Swipe left when you've got a notification on the Lock screen and touch on Manage. Touch Deliver Quietly. Calm notifications come in Notification Centre, but do not show up on the Lock screen, play an audio, present a banner or badge the application icon. You've just surely got to be sure you check every once in a while.

- ***Switch off notifications from an app***: Same method as the "Deliver Quietly" feature, other than you tap the "Switch off..." option.

- ***Open up Notification Centre on Lock screen***: From your lock screen, swipe up from the centre of the screen, and you will visit a long set of earlier notifications if you have any.

- ***Check Notifications anytime***: To check on your Notifications anytime, swipe down from the very best left part of the screen to reveal them.

Using Screen Time

- ***Checking your Screen Time***: You can examine how you've been making use of your phone with the new Screen Time feature in iOS 12. You'll find the reviews in *Configurations > Screen Time.*

- ***Scheduled Downtime:*** If you want just a little help

making use of your mobile phone less, you can restrict what applications you utilize when. Check out Settings > Screen Time and choose the Downtime option. Toggle the change to the "on" position and choose to routine a period when only specific applications and calls are allowed. It's ideal for preventing you or your children from using their cell phones after an arranged time, for example.

- ***Set application limits***: App Limitations enable you to choose which group of applications you want to include a period limit to. Choose the category and then "add" before choosing a period limit and striking "plans."
- ***Choose "always allowed" apps***: However, you might be willing to lock down your phone to avoid

you utilizing it, that's no good if most of your way of getting in touch with people is via an application that gets locked away. Utilize this feature always to allow certain applications whatever limitations you apply.

- ***Content & Personal privacy limitations***: This section is also within the primary Screen Time configurations menu and particularly useful if you are a mother or father with kids who use iOS devices. Utilizing it, you can restrict all types of content and options, including iTunes and in-app buys, location services, advertising, etc. It's worth looking at.

Siri shortcuts

- ***Siri Shortcuts***: There are several little "help" the

iPhone XR offers via Siri Shortcuts. To start to see the ones recommended for you go to Configurations > Siri & Search and choose what you think would be helpful from the automatically produced suggestions. Touch "all shortcuts" to see more. If you wish to install specific “shortcuts” for a variety of different applications that aren’t recommended by the iPhone, you can do this by downloading the dedicated Siri Shortcuts.

iPhone XR: Screen Tips

- ***Standard or Zoomed screen***: Since iPhone 6 Plus, you've had the opportunity to select from two quality options. You can transform the screen settings from Standard or Zoomed on the iPhone

XR too. To change between your two - if you have changed your mind after set up - go to *Configurations > Screen & Lighting > Screen Focus and choose Standard or Zoomed.*

- ***Enable True Tone screen***: If you didn't get it done at the step, you could transform it anytime. To get the iPhone's screen to automatically change its color balance and heat to complement the background light in the area, check out Control Centre and push press the screen lighting slider. Now touch the True Firmness button. You can even go to *Configurations > Screen and Lighting and toggle the "True Shade" switch.*

iPhone XR Photos and Camera Tips

- ***Enable/disable Smart HDR***: Among the new iPhone's camera advancements is HDR, which helps boost colors, light, and detail in hard light conditions. It's on by default, but if you would like to get it turned on or off you manually can check out *Settings > Camera and discover the Smart HDR toggle change.*

- ***Keep a standard photograph with HDR***: Right under the Smart HDR toggle is a "Keep Normal Photo" option, which will save a regular, no HDR version of your picture as well as the Smart HDR photo.

- ***Portrait Lights***: To take Portrait Setting shots with artificial lights, first go to capture in Family portrait mode. Portrait Setting only works together with people on the iPhone XR when capturing with the rear-facing camera. To choose your Portrait Setting capturing style, press and hang on the screen where it says “DAYLIGHT” and then move your finger to the right.

- ***Edit Portrait Lights after taking pictures***: Open up any Family portrait shot in Photos and then tap "edit." After another or two, you will see the light effect icon at the bottom of the image, touch it, and swipe just as you did when shooting the image.

- ***Edit Portrait setting Depth***: Using the new iPhone XR, you can modify the blur impact after shooting the Portrait shot. Check out Photos and choose the picture you want to regulate, then select "edit."

You will see a depth slider at the bottom of the screen. Swipe to boost the blur strength, swipe left to diminish it.

- ***How exactly to Merge People in Photos app***: Photos in iOS can check out your photos and identify people and places. If you discover that the application has chosen the same person, but says they vary, you can combine the albums collectively. To get this done, go directly to the Photos application > Albums and choose People & Places. Touch on the term "Select" at the very top right of the screen and then choose the images of individuals you want to merge, then tap "merge."

- ***Remove people in Photos app***: Head to Photos App, Albums, and choose People & Places. To eliminate tap on "Choose" and then tap on individuals you do not want to see before tapping on "Remove" underneath still left of your iPhone screen.

iPhone XR Control Centre Tips

- ***Add new handles***: Just like the previous version of iOS, you can include and remove handles from Control Centre. Check out *Configurations* > *Control Centre* > *Customise Handles* and then choose which settings you would like to add.
- ***Reorganise handles***: To improve the order of these settings, you've added, touch, and contain the three-bar menu on the right of whichever control you would like to move, then move it along the list

to wherever you would like it to be.

- ***Expand handles***: Some settings may become full screen, press harder on the control you want to expand, and it will fill the screen.
- ***Activate screen recording***: Among the new options, you can include regulating Centre is Screen Recording. Be sure you add the control, then open up Control Centre and press the icon that appears like a good white circle in the thin white band. To any extent further, it'll record everything that occurs on your screen. Press the control again if you are done, and it will save a video to your Photos application automatically.
- ***Adjust light/screen brightness***: You can activate your camera adobe flash, utilizing it as a torch by

starting Control Centre and tapping on the torch icon. If you wish to adjust the lighting, power press the icon, then adapt the full-screen slider that shows up.

- ***Quickly switch where sound is played***: One cool feature is the capability to change where music is playing. While music is playing, through Apple Music, Spotify, or wherever, press on the music control or touch the tiny icon in the very best part of the music control; this introduces a pop-up screening available devices that you can play through; this may be linked earphones, a Bluetooth loudspeaker, Apple Television, your iPhone, or any AirPlay device.

- ***Set an instant timer***: Rather than going to the timer app, you can force press on the timer icon, then glide up or down on the full-screen to create a timer from about a minute to two hours long.

- ***How to gain access to HomeKit devices***: Open up Control Center and then tap on the tiny icon that appears like a home.

iPhone XR Battery Tips

- ***Check your average battery consumption***: In iOS 12, you can check out Settings > Battery, and you will see two graphs. One shows the electric battery level; the other shows your screen on and screen off activity. You will find two tabs. One shows your last day; the other turns up to fourteen days; this way, you can view how energetic your phone battery strength, and breakdowns screening your average screen on and off times show under the graphs.

- ***Enable Low-Power Mode***: The reduced Power Mode (Settings > Electric battery) enables you to reduce power consumption. The feature disables or reduces history application refresh, auto-downloads, email fetch, and more (when allowed). You can turn it on at any point, or you are prompted to carefully turn it on at the 20 and 10 % notification markers. You can even put in control to regulate Centre, and get access to it quickly by swiping up to gain access to Ccontrol Center and tapping on the electric battery icon.

- ***Find electric battery guzzling apps***: iOS specifically lets you know which apps are employing the most power. Head to Configurations > Electric battery and then scroll right down to the section that provides you an in-depth look at all of your battery-guzzling apps.

- ***Check your battery via the Electric battery widget***: Inside the widgets in Today's view, some cards enable you to start to see the battery life staying in your iPhone, Apple Watch, and linked headphones. Just swipe from left to directly on your homescreen to access your Today view and scroll until you start to see the "Batteries" widget.

- ***Charge wirelessly***: To utilize the iPhone's wifi charging capabilities, buy a radio charger. Any Qi charger will continue to work, but to charge more effectively, you will need one optimized for Apple's 7.5W charging.

- ***Fast charge it***: When you have a 29W, 61W, or 87W USB Type-C power adapter for a MacBook, you can plug in your iPhone XS utilizing a Type-C to Lightning wire watching it charge quickly. Up to 50 % in thirty minutes.

iPhone XR: Keyboard Tips

- ***Go one-handed***: iOS 12's QuickType keypad enables you to type one-handed, which is fantastic on the larger devices like the iPhone XR and XS Greatest extent. Press and contain the emoji or world icon and then keypad configurations. Select either the still left or right-sided keypad. It shrinks the keypad and techniques it to 1 aspect of the screen. Get back to full size by tapping the tiny arrow.

- ***Use your keyboard as a trackpad***: Previously, with 3D Touch shows you utilize the keyboard area as a trackpad to go the cursor on screen. You'll still can, but it works just a little in a different way here, rather than pressure pressing anywhere on the keypad, press, and hangs on the spacebar instead.

Face ID Tips

- ***Adding another in-person ID***: if you regularly change appearance now, you can put in a second In person ID to state the iPhone XR getting puzzled. That is also really useful if you would like to add your lover to allow them to use your mobile phone while you're travelling for example.

Chapter 5

How to Fix Common iPhone X Problems

iPhone X Touch Screen Issues

The bright, beautiful ***"edge-to-edge"*** OLED screen on the iPhone is one of its major new features; however, the touch screen may sometimes go wrong. Both most common situations are:

- ✓ ***Non-responsive SCREEN AND "GHOST TOUCHES."***

Some users state that the screen on the iPhone X sometimes halts working. In those instances, the screen doesn't react to details or touches. In other situations, the contrary occurs: "ghost details" appear to activate things on the screen even when they don't touch it.

If you are experiencing either of these issues, the reason

is the same: a hardware problem with the touch screen chips and detectors in the iPhone X; because these problems are the effect of a hardware issue, you can't fix them yourself. Fortunately, Apple knows the problem and offers to repair it. Find out about how to proceed on Apple's web page about the problem.

✓ ***FROZEN Screen IN WINTER***

A different type of iPhone X screen problem that many people run into would be that the screen freezes up and becomes unresponsive for a couple of seconds when going from a warm spot to a chilly one (such as moving out into a wintery day). The good thing is that this is not a hardware problem, so it is much simpler to fix. Try out these quick DIY fix:

- *Update the iOS*: This issue was set with the iOS 11.1.2 update, so make sure you're operating that version of the operating system or higher.

- *Follow Apple's Cold-Weather Recommendations*: Apple has tips and recommendations for the temperatures to use the iPhone in, it suggests not using it in temperature ranges less than 32 degrees F (0 degrees C). Having your iPhone within your clothes and near to your body, warmth is an excellent, simple fix.

iPhone X Screen Issues

The iPhone X was the first iPhone to use the brighter, better OLED screen technology. The screen appears excellent, but it's susceptible to some issues that other iPhones using different systems aren't. Perhaps most obviously among these is "burn off in."; this happens when the same image is shown on a screen for an extended period, resulting in faint "spirits" of these images showing up on the screen regularly, regardless of what else has been screened. Fortunately, OLED burn-in is simple to avoid. Just follow these pointers:

- *Lower Screen Lighting*: The low the lighting of your screen, the less likely a graphic burn off involved with it. You have two options here. First, you can by hand reduce your screen brightness by starting Control Center and moving the lighting slider down. On the other hand, let your screen brightness change to ambient light by heading to *Configurations -> General -> Convenience -> Screen brightness -> Auto-Brightness*.

- *Set Screen to Auto-Lock*: Burn off happens when a graphic is on the screen for an extended period. So, if your screen hair and shuts off regularly, the image can't burn off. Set your screen to lock by heading to Configurations automatically -> Screen & Lighting -> Auto-Lock and choose five minutes or less.

Another screen problem that impacts some iPhone X models is a green line that appears at the right edge of the screen. That is another hardware problem that users can't fix themselves. If you see this, your very best wager is to get hold of Apple to get active support.

iPhone X Face ID Problems

Most likely, the single coolest feature of the iPhone X is the facial ID, the facial recognition system. This feature is utilized for security and convenience: it unlocks the telephone, can be used to enter passwords, and even authorizes Apple Pay transactions. But issues with Face ID and either front or back camera can cause your iPhone X never to identify you. If you are (ahem) facing this issue, try these pointers:

- *Adjust iPhone Position*: If Face ID sometimes identifies you, but other times doesn't, consider changing the position you're holding the telephone. As the Face ID sensors are relatively sophisticated, they need to be capable of getting a good view of that person to work.

- *Clean "The Notch."*: THE FACIAL ID detectors are situated in "the notch," the deep cut-out near the top of the screen. If those receptors get protected with dirt or even enough oil from your skin layer, their standard procedure could be reduced. Try wiping "the notch" clean.

- *Update the OS*: Apple regularly enhances the speed and precision of Face ID, as well as fixes insects, in new variations of the iOS. If you are having Face ID problems on iPhone X, make sure you're using the latest operating system.

- *Reset Face ID*: The problem is probably not with Face ID itself, but instead with the initial scans of that person created when you set up Face ID to start. If the other activities haven't helped, be rid of your old face scans and make new ones. Enter a shiny, well-lit place and then go to Configurations -> Face ID & Passcode -> enter your passcode -> Reset Face ID. Then create Face ID from scratch.

- *Contact Apple*: If none of the things has helped,

there may be a problem with the hardware in your iPhone X (maybe it's a problem with the video cameras, the Face ID sensors, or another thing). If so, you should contact Apple to obtain an analysis of the problem and a fix.

- *You might have seen tales on the internet claiming that Face ID has been hacked*: They are virtually all bogus. Face ID can be an extremely advanced system that depends on thousands of data factors to identify a face. Yes, similar twins might be able to beat Face ID (it seems sensible; they have simply the same face!). Other families that look nearly the same as one another can also be able to technique it. But also, for the most part, the probability of Face ID being tricked or hacked is very, surprisingly low.

iPhone X Loudspeaker Problems

The iPhone is a great multimedia device; however, many users report reduced enjoyment of media on the iPhone X credited to speaker problems. Listed below are two of the very most common.

a) SPEAKERS Audio MUFFLED

Speakers whose audio is quiet than they ought to, or whose audio sounds muffled, can frequently be fixed by doing the next:

- *Restart iPhone*: Restarting your iPhone can solve all types of problems, including sound issues.
- *Clean the Speakers*. You might have dirt or other gunk developed on the loudspeakers that are leading to the quietness. Understand how to completely clean iPhone speakers.

- *Check the Case*: If you are using a case with your iPhone, make sure there is nothing stuck between your case and the loudspeaker, like pocket lint, that may be causing the problem.

b) Loudspeaker CRACKLES at high volume

Around the other end of the range, some iPhone X users have reported that their speakers make a distressing crackling sound when their volume is too high. If this is going on for you, try the next steps:

- *Restart iPhone*: It might not assist in this case, but it's fast and straightforward so that it never hurts to get one of this restart. You can also get one of these hard reset if you want.

- *Update the OS*: Because the latest version of the iOS also includes the latest bug fixes, make sure you're operating it.

- *Talk with Apple*: Crackling loudspeakers are likely to be always a hardware problem that you can't solve. Get active support from Apple instead.

Some individuals have encountered problems using Wi-Fi on the iPhone X. This probably isn't a concern with the iPhone X itself. Much more likely, this has regarding software configurations or your Wi-Fi network. Find out about the complexities and fixes in How exactly to Fix an iPhone That Can't Hook up to Wi-Fi in other recommended books at the end of this book.

iPhone X Charging Problems

The iPhone X is the first iPhone to add support for

wireless charging. That's cool, but it isn't cool if the telephone won't charge properly. If you are facing that problem, try these steps to repair it:

- ***Get one of these New Charging Wire***: Maybe the charging problem has been your wire, not your phone. Try another wire you know for certain works. Make especially certain to either use the official Apple wire or one that's qualified by Apple.

- ***Remove Credit cards From Case***: If you are wanting to charge cellular and have an instance that also stores things such as credit cards, take away the credit cards. The cellular payment top features of the credit cards can hinder the cellular charging.

- ***Remove Case for Wifi Charging***: Removing the whole case may be considered a good idea if you are charging wirelessly. Not absolutely all cases are appropriate for cellular charging, so that they may be avoiding normal function.

- ***Restart iPhone***: You never know very well what types of problems a restart can solve. This may be one of them.

iPhone X Electric battery Life Problems

There is nothing worse than not having the ability to use your mobile phone because it's working out of electric battery too early, but that's the thing some users complain about. And with most of its fresh, power-hungry features - the OLED screen, for example - it isn't a shock that there could be some iPhone X electric battery problems.

Fortunately, battery issues on the iPhone are simple enough to solve using the settings included in iOS.

Below are a few tips:

- ***Learn to Preserve Battery***: There are over 30+ tips about how to raise your iPhone's electric battery life. Use a few of these as well as your iPhone would run much longer between charges.

- ***Update the OS***: Furthermore, to fix a bug, new variations of iOS often deliver improvements that make the battery better. Install the latest revise, and you'll see your electric battery last longer.

- ***Get a protracted Life Electric battery***: Maybe the simplest way to get your electric battery to go longer is to obtain additional battery. There are sorts of prolonged life batteries on the marketplace, from exterior dongles to others.

CHAPTER 6

How to Set-up and Restore iPhone X Series Backup from iCloud and iTunes

There is no need connecting your brand-new iPhone X Series to your personal computer, as long as there is a mobile data connection designed for activation. As you end the set-up wizard, you may navigate back by tapping the back arrow at the top left-hand side of the screen and scroll further to another display by tapping another button at the top right-hand corner.

You can commence by pressing down the power button at the top edge of your brand-new iPhone X Series. You may want to keep it pressed down for about two seconds until you notice a vibration, meaning the iPhone X Series is booting up.

Once it boots up finally, you can start initial set up by following the processes below;

- Swipe your finger over the display screen to start the set-up wizard.
- Choose the language of preference - English is usually at the top of the list, so there is no problem finding it. However, if you would like to apply a different language, scroll down to look for your desired language, and tap to select the preferred language.
- Choose your country - United States may be near the top of the list. If otherwise, scroll down the list and select the United States or any of your choice.
- You need to connect your iPhone X Series to the internet to start its activation. You can test this via a link with a Wi-Fi network. Locate the name of

your available network in the list shown, and then tap on it to select it.

- Enter the Wi-Fi security password (you will generally find this written on your router, which is probably known as the WPA Key, WEP Key, or Password) and select Sign up. A tick indication shows you are connected, and a radio image appears near the top of the screen. The iPhone X Series will now start activation with Apple automatically. This may take some time!
- In case your iPhone X Series is a 4G version, you will be requested to check for updated internet configurations after inserting a new Sim card. You can test this anytime, so, for the present time, tap **Continue**.
- Location services will help you with mapping, weather applications, and more, giving you

specific information centered wholly on what your location is. Select whether to use location service by tapping allow location services.

- You would now be requested to create **Touch ID,** which is Apple's fingerprint identification. **Touch ID** allows you to unlock your iPhone X Series with your fingerprint instead of your passcode or security password. To set up Tap Identification, put a finger or your thumb on the home button (but do not press it down!). To by-pass this for the moment, tap ***setup Tap Identification later***.
- If you are establishing Touch ID, the tutorial instruction on the screen will walk you through the set-up process. Put your finger on the home button, then remove it till the iPhone X Series has properly scanned your fingerprint. Whenever your print is wholly scanned, you will notice a screen letting

you know that tap recognition is successful. Tap **Continue**.

- You will be requested to enter a passcode to secure your iPhone X Series. If you create **Touch ID**, you must use a passcode if in any case your fingerprint isn't acknowledged. Securing your computer data is an excellent idea, and the iPhone X Series provides you with several options. Tap password option to choose your lock method.
- You can arrange a Custom Alphanumeric Code (that is a security password that uses characters and figures), a Custom Numeric Code (digit mainly useful, however, you can add as many numbers as you want!) or a 4-Digit Numeric Code (a high old college pin!). In case you didn't install or setup **Touch ID** you may even have an option not to add a Security password. Tap on your

selected Security option.

- I would recommend establishing a 4-digit numeric code, or Touch ID for security reasons, but all optional setup is done likewise. Input your selected Security password using the keyboard.
- Verify your Security password by inputting it again. If the Password does not match, you'll be requested to repeat! If indeed they do match, you'll continue to another display automatically.

At this time of the set-up process, you'll be asked whether you have used an iPhone X Series before and probably upgrading it, you can restore all of your applications and information from an iCloud or iTunes backup by deciding on the best option. If this is your first iPhone X Series, you will have to get it started as new, yet, in case you are moving from Android to an iPhone X

Series, you can transfer all your data by deciding and choosing the choice you want.

How to Restore iPhone X Series Back-up from iCloud or iTunes

If you want to restore your iPhone X Series from an iTunes back-up, you may want to connect to iCloud and have the latest version of iTunes installed on it. If you are ready to begin this process, tap **restore** from iTunes back-up on your iPhone X Series and connect it to your personal computer. Instructions about how to bring back your data can be followed on the laptop screen.

In case your old iPhone X Series was supported on iCloud, then follow the instructions below to restore your applications & data to your brand-new device:

- Tap ***Restore*** from iCloud back-up.
- Register with the Apple ID and Password that you applied to your old iPhone X Series. If you fail to recollect the security password, there's a link that may help you reset it.
- The Terms & Conditions screen will show. Tap the links to learn about specific areas in detail. When you are ready to proceed, select **Agree**.
- Your iPhone X Series will need some moments to create your Apple ID and hook up with the iCloud server.
- You will notice a summary of available backups to download. The most up-to-date backup will be observed at the very top, with almost every other reserve below it. If you want to restore from a desirable backup, tap the screen for ***all backups*** to see the available choices.

- Tap on the back-up you want to restore to start installing.
- A progress bar will be shown, providing you with a demo of the advancement of the download. When the restore is completed, the device will restart.
- You would see a notification telling you that your iPhone X Series is updated effectively. Tap ***Continue***.
- To complete the iCloud set up on your recently restored iPhone X Series, you should re-enter your iCloud (Apple ID) password. Enter/review it and then tap ***Next***.
- You'll be prompted to upgrade the security information related to your ***Apple ID***. Tap on any stage to replace your computer data, or even to

bypass this option. If you aren't ready to do this, then tap the ***Next*** button.

- **Apple pay** is Apple's secure payment system that stores encrypted credit or debit card data on your device and making use of your iPhone X Series also with your fingerprint to make safe transactions online and with other apps. Select ***Next*** to continue.
- To ***feature/add a card***, place it on a set surface and place the iPhone X Series over it, so the card is put in the camera framework. The credit card info will be scanned automatically, and you will be requested to verify that the details on display correspond with your card. You'll also be asked to enter the ***CVV*** (safety code) from the personal strip behind the card. If you choose (or the camera cannot recognize your cards), you can enter credit

card information by hand by tapping the hyperlink. You could bypass establishing **Apple Pay** by tapping ***create later***.

- Another screen discusses the ***iCloud keychain***, which is Apple's secure approach to sharing your preserved security password and payment information throughout all your Apple devices. You might use *iCloud security code* to validate your brand-new device and import present data, or you might be asked to continue registering your keychain if it's your first Apple device. In case you don't want to share vital data with other devices, you should go to *avoid iCloud keychain* or *don't restore passwords*.
- If you selected to set up your Apple keychain, you'll be notified to either use a Security password (the same one you'd set up on your iPhone X

Series) or produce a different code. If you're making use of your iCloud security code, you should put it on your iPhone X Series when prompted.

- This will confirm your ID when signing on to an iCloud safety code; a confirmation code will be delivered via SMS. You may want to hyperlink your smartphone text code (if you have never distributed one with Apple already) so that the code may be provided as a text. Then enter this code to your iPhone X Series if requested, then select ***Next.***
- You'll then be asked to create **Siri**. ***Siri*** is your own digital personal associate, which might search the internet, send communications, and check out data in your device and a lot more, all without having to flick via specific apps. Choose to create

Siri by tapping the choice or start Siri later to skip this task for now.

- To set up and create SIRI, you will need to speak several phrases to the iPhone X Series to review your conversation patterns and identify your voice.
- Once you say every term, a tick will be observed, showing that it's been known and comprehended. Another phrase may indicate that you should read aloud.
- Once you've completed the five phrases, you will notice a display notifying that Siri has been set up correctly. Tap ***Continue***.
- The iPhone X Series display alters the color balance to help make the screen show up naturally under distinctive light conditions. You can switch this off in the screen settings after the iPhone X

Series has completed configuring it. Tap ***continue*** to continue with the setup.

- Has your iPhone X Series been restored? Tap begin to transfer your computer data to your brand-new iPhone X Series.
- You'll be prompted to ensure your brand-new iPhone X Series has enough power to avoid the device turning off in the process of downloading applications and information. Tap ***OK*** to verify this recommendation.
- You will notice a notification show up on your apps, to download in the background.

How to Move Data From an Android Phone

Apple has made it quite easy to move your data from a Google Android device to your new iPhone X Series.

Proceed to the iOS app. I'll direct you about how to use the application to move your data!

- Using the iPhone X Series, if you are on the applications & data screen of the set-up wizard, tap ***move data from Google android***.
- Go to the Play Store on your Google android device and download the app recommended by the set-up wizard. When it is installed, open up the app, select **Continue** and you'll be shown the ***Terms & Conditions*** to continue.
- On your Android device, tap ***Next*** to start linking your Devices. On your own iPhone X Series, select ***Continue***.
- Your iPhone X Series will show a 6-digit code which has to be received into the **Google android** device to set the two phone up.

- Your Google android device will screen all the data that'll be moved. By default, all options are ticked - so if there could be something you don't want to move, tap the related collection to deselect it. If you are prepared to continue, tap ***Next*** on your Google android device.
- As the change progresses, you will notice the iPhone X Series display screen changes, showing you the position of the info transfer and progress report.
- When the transfer is completed, you will notice a confirmation screen on each device. On your Android Device, select ***Done*** to shut the app. On your own iPhone X Series, tap ***Continue Installing iPhone X Series***.
- An Apple ID allows you to download apps, supported by your iPhone X Series and

synchronize data through multiple devices, which makes it an essential account you should have on your iPhone X Series! If you have been using an iPhone X Series previously, or use iTunes to download music to your laptop, then you should have already become an Apple ID user. Register with your username and passwords (when you have lost or forgotten your Apple ID or password you will see a link that may help you reset it). If you're not used to iPhone X Series, select doesn't have an Apple ID to create one for free.

- The Terms & Conditions for your iPhone X Series can be seen. Please go through them (tapping on more to study additional info), so when you are done, tap ***Agree***.
- You'll be asked about synchronizing your data with iCloud. That's to ensure bookmarks,

connections and other items of data are supported securely with your other iPhone X Series's data. Tap ***merge*** to permit this or ***don't merge*** if you'll have a choice to keep your details elsewhere asides iCloud.

- **Apple pay** is Apple's secure payment system that stores encrypted credit or debit card data on your device and making use of your iPhone X Series also with your fingerprint to make safe transactions online and with other apps. Select ***Next*** to continue.
- To ***feature/add a card***, place it on a set surface and place the iPhone X Series over it, so the card is put in the camera framework. The credit card info will be scanned automatically, and you will be requested to verify that the details on display correspond with your card. You'll also be asked to

enter the ***CVV*** (safety code) from the personal strip behind the card. If you choose (or the camera cannot recognize your cards), you can enter credit card information by hand by tapping the hyperlink. You could bypass establishing **Apple Pay** by tapping ***create later***.

- Another screen discusses ***iCloud keychain***, which is Apple's secure approach to sharing your preserved security password and payment information throughout all your Apple devices. You might use *iCloud security code* to validate your brand-new device and import present data, or you might be asked to continue registering your keychain if it's your first Apple device. In case you don't want to share vital data with other devices, you should go to *avoid iCloud keychain* or *don't restore passwords*.

- If you selected to set up your Apple keychain, you'll be notified to either use a Security password (the same one you'd set up on your iPhone X Series) or produce a different code. If you're making use of your iCloud security code, you should put it on your iPhone X Series when prompted.
- This will confirm your ID when signing on to an iCloud safety code; a confirmation code will be delivered via SMS. You may want to hyperlink your smartphone text code (if you have never distributed one with Apple already) so that the code may be provided as a text. Then enter this code to your iPhone X Series if requested, then select ***Next.***
- You'll then be asked to create **Siri**. ***Siri*** is your own digital personal associate, which might search

the internet, send communications, and check out data in your device and a lot more, all without having to flick via specific apps. Choose to create Siri by tapping the choice or start Siri later to skip this task for now.

- To set up and create SIRI, you will need to speak several phrases to the iPhone X Series to review your conversation patterns and identify your voice.
- Once you say every term, a tick will be observed, showing that it's been known and comprehended. Another phrase may indicate that you should read aloud.
- Once you've completed the five phrases, you will notice a display notifying that Siri has been set up correctly. Tap ***Continue***.
- The iPhone X Series display alters the color

balance to help make the screen show up naturally under distinctive light conditions. You can switch this off in the screen settings after the iPhone X Series has completed configuring it. Tap ***continue*** to continue with the setup.

- Has your iPhone X Series been restored? Tap begin to transfer your computer data to your brand-new iPhone X Series.
- You'll be prompted to ensure your brand-new iPhone X Series has enough power to avoid the device turning off in the process of downloading applications and information. Tap ***OK*** to verify this recommendation.
- You will notice a notification show up on your apps, to download in the background.

NB: *Setting up a new iPhone X Series: Similar method, as described above, applies.*

Chapter 7

Ways of Creating and Using iPhone X Series Shortcuts

How to Put in a Virtual Home Button to the iPhone

In respect to get a virtual Home button configured, you first have to allow the home button itself. Here's how:

- Touch *Settings*.
- Touch *General*.
- Touch *Accessibility*.
- Touch *AssistiveTouch*.
- Move the *AssistiveTouch* slider to On/green. The digital Home button shows up on your screen.

- Position the button anywhere on your screen using drag and drop.
- Make the button pretty much transparent utilizing the Idle Opacity slider.
- Touch the button to see its default menu.

<u>How to Customize the Virtual Home Button Menu</u>

To change the number of shortcuts and the precise ones that exist in the default menu:

- Around the *Assistive Touch* screen, tap Customize Top Level Menu.
- Change the number of icons shown in the very best Level Menu with the plus and minus control keys at the bottom of the screen. The minimum volume

of options is 1; the utmost is 8. Each icon represents a different shortcut.

- To improve a shortcut, touch the icon you want to improve.
- Tap one of the available shortcuts from the list that appears.
- Touch Done to save the change. It replaces the shortcut you have chosen.
- If you decide you want to return to the default group of options, touch Reset.

How to Add Custom Activities to the Virtual Home Button

Now that you understand how to include the virtual

Home button and configure the menu, it is time to get to the nice stuff: custom shortcuts. As being a physical Home button, the digital button can be configured to react differently based about how you touch it. Some tips about what you must do:

Within the AssistiveTouch screen, go directly to the Custom Actions section. For that section, touch the action that you would like to use to result in the new shortcut. Your alternatives are:

- ***Single-Touch***: The original single click of the home button. In cases like this, it's an individual touch on the digital button.
- ***Double-Touch***: Two quick touchs on the button; if you choose this, you can also control the Timeout establishing (i.e., the time allowed between touches) if additional time goes by between

touches, the iPhone goodies them as two solitary touches, not a double-touch.

- ***Long Press***: Touch and contain the virtual Home button. If you choose this, you can also configure a Duration, which sets how long you will need to press the screen because of this feature to be triggered.

- ***3D Touch***: The 3D Touch screen on modern iPhones lets the screen respond differently based on how hard you press it. Utilize this option to have the digital Home button react to hard presses.

Whichever action you touch, each screen presents several options for shortcuts that you can assign to the action. They are especially cool because they change actions that may normally require pressing multiple control keys into an individual touch.

Most shortcuts are self-explanatory, such as Siri, Screenshot, or Volume Up, but a few need description:

- ***Convenience Shortcut***: This shortcut may be used to cause all types of convenience features, such as inverting colors for users with eyesight impairment, turning on VoiceOver, and zooming in on the screen.
- ***Shaking***: Choose this, and the iPhone responds to a button touch as if an individual shook the telephone. Shake pays for undoing certain activities, particularly if physical issues prevent you from shaking the telephone.
- ***Pinch***: Performs the same as a pinch gesture on the

iPhone's screen, which pays for people who've impairments that produce pinching hard or impossible.

- ***SOS***: This button allows the iPhone's Emergency SOS feature, which causes a loud sound to alert others that you might need help and a call to Emergency services.

- ***Analytics***: This feature starts the gathering of Assistive Touch diagnostics.

Chapter 8

Top Best iPhone X Apps for Year 2020

Spark: Best Email App for iPhone X

If you center on iOS apps, you would understand that email has taken on something similar to the role of the antagonist in the wonderful world of iOS. App designers appear to know that everyone needs a better email platform, and they want an application to resolve their issues. Controlling email is just a little less stressful if you are using ***Spark*** as you would find features to suit your needs such as; sending, snoozing email messages, and a good inbox that only notifies you of important email messages.

Below are the things you'd like about this application:

- The app is simple to use and social friendly.

- Swipe-based interaction allows for one-handed operation.

What You may not like about it:

- No filter systems for automatically sorting email messages.
- The app does not have a way of controlling messages in batches.

***Things**: The best "To-do manager" for the iPhone X*

To-do manager applications are a packed field, and the application called ***"Things"*** isn't the only good one, and it is also not the only *to-do manager* on this list, but it's a carefully reliable tool, seated between control and hardy. The application provides the ideal levels of both control and hardy, without mind-boggling users to dials and without dropping essential features.

Things you'd like about this application:

- This app has a simplified interface that reduces stress when adding and completing the task.
- Tasks can be added from iOS with the sheet extension.

What you may not like are:

- Repeating tasks and deadlines can be buggy.
- Tasks can't be put into the calendar automatically.

***OmniCenter*: Best GTD-compatible To-Do App for iPhone X**

Like *"Things"*, ***OmniCenter*** is a favorite and well-designed to-do manager; however, they have a different group of priorities. Where ***Things*** attempts to remain simple and straightforward, ***OmniCenter*** is feature-rich and robust.

The application fully integrates with the ***"Getting Things Done"*** approach to task management called **GTD**, and this method stimulates users to jot down any duties they have, as well as almost all their associated information and scheduling. GTD users would finish up spending a great deal of time on leading end arranging work; because of this, the software takes a robust feature collection to implement all areas of the GTD process.

Things you'd like about this application:

- Most effective to-do list manager available.
- Can participate in virtually any task management

style.

What you may not like:

- Sacrifices simpleness and usability for power and versatility.

***Agenda*: Best iPhone X App for Busy Notice Takers**

Agenda requires a different spin on the notes application than almost every other applications; its also known as *"date centred notice taking app."* Records are structured by task and day, and the times are a large part of the Agenda. Instead of merely collecting your jotting into a collection, Agenda creates a to-do list from *"things"*, with tight time integration, Agenda makes an operating journaling app and an able to-do manager and general iPhone X note-taking app. The day and note mixture seems apparent, but Agenda is the first iOS note-taking application to perform this mixture effectively.

It's a "to-do manager" and also a note-taking application with some calendar features, which enables seeing every information in a single place with one perspective and only one app. The application is also highly practical in the freeform, which may be uncommon in flagship apps. The beauty of the app ***"Agenda"*** comes out when using with Pencil support, but for the present time, we'll have to turn to the iPad Pro for the feature.

Things you'd like about this application:

- Note-taking small tweaks can improve many workflows.
- The time-based organization fits most users'

mental types of information organization.

What you may not like:

- Slow app release can limit how quickly you can write down a note.

***1Password**: Best iPhone X App for Security password Management*

Using the auto-fill in iOS 12, ***1Password*** is as near to perfect as we have in a password manager. The Face ID authentication isn't unique to the iPhone X alone, but access Face ID makes the application better and simpler to use, which is an uncommon combination of accomplishments to reach concurrently.

Things you'd like about this application:

- Finding and copying usernames and passwords is extremely easy.

- Secure document storage space means *1Password* can gather all of your secure information in a single place.

- Auto-fill support finally makes security password management as easy as typing your security password.

What you may not like:

- No free version.

- The paid version uses membership pricing.

***Twitterific*: Best Tweets App For iPhone X**

Twitter is probably not the most exceptional sociable media system, but it's still one of the very most popular internet sites around, and like many internet sites, Twitter's default application is disappointingly bad.

Unfortunately, Twitter does lately nerf third-party Twitter clients. Third-party applications won't receive real-time stream notifications, significantly reducing the effectiveness of the applications; this move seems to pressure users to go to the native app, but considering its many defects, Twitterific and applications like it remain better.

Things you'd like about this application:

- Improves Twitter's visual demonstration dramatically.
- Includes smart and powerful features that make Twitter simpler to use.

What you may not like:

- Some organisational options are unintuitive initially.
- Twitter has purposefully knee-capped a good number of third-party apps, and Twitterific is no defence to those results.

<u>Overcast</u>: Best iPhone X App for Podcasts

Overcast is the best application you may use to hear podcasts. The app's user interface is carefully considered for maximal consumer performance, with features like “Smart Rate” which helps to intelligently manages a podcast's playback velocity to shorten silences without accelerating speech, while Tone of voice Boost offers a pre-built EQ curve made to amplify voices, which is ideal for a loud hearing environment.

Things you'd like about this application:

- Thoughtfully designed interface for sorting and hearing podcasts.
- Features like Smart Velocity and Queue playlists are invaluable once you're used to them.
- Active developer centred on avoiding an unhealthy user experience concerning monetization.

What you may not like;

- It most definitely doesn't seem to go nicely with the iOS lock screen.

***Apollo*: Best iPhone X App for Reddit**

If you're thinking about *Reddit*, you would want to see the website beyond the third-party app. The application has improved, sure, but it's still kilometres behind third-party offerings.

Apollo is the best of the number as it pertains to Reddit clients, conquering out past champions like "Narwhal." Development is continuous and ongoing, with many improvements from the dev in the app's subreddit.

The swipe-based navigation would continue to work on any iPhone, of course, but it dovetails nicely with the iPhone X's application switching behaviour. The real black setting is also a delicacy for OLED screens.

Things you'd like about this application:

- Effortlessly handles an enormous variety of media.
- Well developed UI makes navigation easy.
- No ads in virtually any version of the app.

What you may not like:

- Sometimes is suffering from annoying and lingering bugs.

***Focos*: Best iPhone X App for Editing and enhancing Portrait Setting Photos**

By default, the iPhone X's Family portrait Mode is a one-and-done process; you take the picture, and the blur is applied. iOS doesn't give a built-in way for editing and enhancing the Picture Setting effect following the fact. Focos fills the space, creating a tool to tweak both degrees of shadow and the blur face mask. It mimics the result you'd see when modifying a zoom lens' physical aperture. More magically, you can also change the centre point following the shot by recreating the blurred cover up on the different object, or by hand adjusting the result on the image's depth face mask instantly.

Things you'd like about this application:

- The most effective approach to manipulating Portrait Mode's depth-of-field effect.
- The depth map is a distinctive feature to help visualize blur.

What you may not like:

- Simple to make images look over-processed.
- Only about the centre, 50% of the blur range looks natural.

Halide: Best iPhone X App for Natural Photos

Distinctively, *Halide* sticks important info in the iPhone X's "ear." It embeds a live histogram for image evaluation; could it be precious? Nearly, but Halide is a near-perfect picture taking software besides that offering feature.

The settings are ideally positioned and configured, the RAW catch is pixel-perfect, and navigation within the application is easy and immediately understandable. If you are seriously interested in taking photos on your iPhone X, *Halide* is the best camera application for iOS.

Things you'd like about this application:

- Deep handling power for iPhone photos.
- Broadest toolset of any iOS image editing and enhancing the app.

What you may not like:

- It is able to overwhelm first-time users using its degree of control.

***Euclidean Lands**: The Top-rated AR Puzzle Game for iPhone X*

Augmented reality applications haven't yet found their killer use. But AR gambling takes great benefit from lots of the iPhone X's features.

Euclidean Lands is a brief fun puzzler that calls for the full benefit of AR's potential. Similar to Monument Valley, players manipulate the play space to produce new pathways through puzzle designs, guiding their avatar to the finish of the maze. The overall game begins easy; nevertheless, you might be scratching your head just a little by the end.

Things you'd like in this application:

- Challenging and attractive puzzle levels that take benefit of AR's unique features.

What you may not like:

- Disappointingly short.
- Core game auto technician feels very familiar.

Giphy World: Best AR Messaging App for iPhone X

Plenty of applications have tried to usurp Snapchat as an AR messaging system. While Snapchat might maintain a weakened condition because of self-inflicted damage, it isn't eliminated yet. But if it can decrease, Giphy World is a great replacement.

Things you'd like about this application:

- Simple to create fun and funny images from provided assets.
- Content isn't locked inside the Giphy app.

What you may not like:

- Object place and processing speed are inferior compared to Snapchat's.

***Jig Space*: Best Usage of AR for Education on iPhone X**

Learning with holograms is one particular thing you constantly see in sci-fi movies; with ***Jig Space*** and ***augmented*** actuality, that kind of thing is now possible in our daily lives. You should use the application to find out about various topics, including what sort of lock works, manipulating every part of the system, and looking at it from alternative perspectives. Jig Space requires benefit of AR's three sizes effectively, and the low-poly models AR has bound to not harm the grade of the visualizations.

Things you'd like about this application:

- Takes benefit of AR's advantages for a good cause.
- A substantial assortment of "jigs" charges is free.

What you may not like:

- Accompanying captions are occasionally disappointingly shallow.

Nighttime Sky: Best Late-Night Outside Companion App

Directing out constellations is much more fun if you are not making them up as you decide to go. *Evening Sky* was main augmented-reality style application to seem on iOS. It shows just how for others on the system wanting to mimic its success, but it's remained dominant nevertheless.

Things you'd like about this application:

- Enhances the natural world with technology.
- Improves the star-gazing experience for both children and adults.

What you may not like:

- Large image units mean large camera motions are stiff and jerky.

***Inkhunter**: MOST READILY USEFUL AR Gimmick on iOS*

There's something distinctively exotic about checking out new tattoos by yourself. *Inkhunter* uses the energy of augmented truth to generate short-term digital tattoos you can construct on the body and screenshot. You should use the built-in adobe flash, pull your designs, or import property from somewhere else to project on your skin.

Things you'd like about this application:

- Fun and book application idea that's useful.

What you may not like:

- Is suffering from AR's existing restrictions in surface matching.

Chapter 9

How to Restart an iPhone (All Models)

The iPhone is a robust computer that ties in a pocket. As being a pc or laptop, sometimes an iPhone must be restarted or reset to repair a problem. To restart an iPhone, transform it off, then transform it on. When an iPhone doesn't react to a restart, execute a reset. Neither process deletes the info or configurations on the iPhone. These aren't exactly like a restore, which erases all this content on the iPhone and returning it to manufacturing conditions, and you restore your computer data from a back-up.

How to Restart the iPhone XR, iPhone XS, iPhone X, and iPhone 8 (Plus)

Restart an iPhone to resolve fundamental problems, such as poor cellular or Wi-Fi connectivity, application crashes, or other day-to-day glitches. On these models, Apple designated new functions to the *Rest/Wake button* privately of these devices. It could be used to activate *Siri*, talk about the Emergency SOS feature, or other tasks. As a result of this change, the restart process differs from the technique used in previous models.

To restart an iPhone XR, iPhone XS, iPhone X, and iPhone 8:

- Press and contain the Rest/Wake and Volume Down buttons at the same time. Volume up works, too, but utilizing it can unintentionally have a screenshot.

- When the slide to power off slider shows up, release the Rest/Wake and Volume Down buttons.
- Move the slider from left to shut down the phone.

How to Restart Other iPhone Models

Restarting other iPhone models is equivalent to turning the iPhone On/Off. Some tips about what to do:

- ***Press and contain the Rest/Wake button***: On old models, it's at the top of the phone. on the iPhone 6 series and newer, it's on the right part.
- When the power off slider appears on the screen, release the Rest/Wake button.

- ***Move the power off slider from left to right***: This gesture prompts the iPhone to turn off. A spinner shows on the screen indicating the shutdown is happening. It might be dim and hard to see.

- When the phone shuts off, press and contain the *Rest/Wake button*.

- When the Apple logo design appears on the screen, release the *Sleep/Wake button*, and await the iPhone to complete restarting.

How to Precisely Hard Reset the iPhone XR, iPhone XS, iPhone X, and iPhone 8

The essential restart solves many problems, but it generally does not solve all of them. In a few cases such as when the phone is completely freezing and won't react to pressing the Rest/Wake button, a better option called a

hard reset is necessary.

On iPhone XS or XR, iPhone X, and iPhone 8 series, the hard reset process differs from other models. To hard reset these iPhone models:

- Click and release the Volume Up button.
- Click and release the Volume down button.
- Press and contain the Rest/Wake button before gliding to power off slider appears.
- Move the slip to force off slider from left to reset the phone.

How to Hard Reset Other iPhone Models

A hard reset restarts the phone and refreshes the memory space that applications run in. It generally does not delete data but normally helps the iPhone begin from scratch. Generally, a hard reset is not needed, however when it is necessary on a mature model (except iPhone 7), follow these steps:

- With the phone screen facing you, press down the Sleep/Wake button and the home button at exactly the same time.
- Continue to contain the control keys when the power off slider shows up, don't release the control keys.
- When the Apple logo design appears, release the Sleep/Wake button and the home button.
- Wait as the iPhone resets.

How to Hard Reset iPhone 7 Series

The hard reset process is somewhat different for the

iPhone 7 series. That's because the home button is not a physical button on these models; it's a 3D Touch -panel. Because of this, Apple transformed how these models are reset.

Using the iPhone 7 series, keep the Volume Down button pressed, and the Sleep/Wake button at exactly the same time.

For more Help Resetting Your iPhone

Sometimes an iPhone may have problems so complicated a restart or reset doesn't work. Follow these advanced troubleshooting steps to fix the problem:

- ***Stuck at Apple Logo***: If an iPhone is stuck at the Apple logo during startup, a straightforward restart might not be adequate to solve the problem. I recommend taking the iPhone to a professional or Apple repair center.

- ***Restore to Manufacturing default Settings***: If you wish to erase all the info from an iPhone and begin from inception; this solves some hard bugs. Before you sell your iPhone, restore it to factory settings.
- ***Recovery Setting***: If an iPhone is stuck in a reboot loop or can't see through the Apple logo design during startup, try iPhone recovery mode.
- ***DFU Mode***: When downgrading the version of the iOS or jailbreak the phone, use DFU (Disk Firmware Update) mode.

Chapter 10

iPhone X Home Button Basics

Possibly the biggest change Apple introduced using its groundbreaking iPhone X was removing the home button. Because of the iPhone's debut, the home button has been the only button on leading the phone. It had also been the most crucial button since it was used to come back to the home screen, to gain access to multitasking, to consider screenshots, plus much more.

You can still do all those things on the iPhone X, but how you need to do them differs. Pressing a button has been changed by a couple of new gestures that result in those familiar functions. Continue reading to learn all the gestures that changed the home button on the iPhone X.

How to Unlock the iPhone X

Waking the iPhone X from sleep, also called unlocking the phone (never to be puzzled with unlocking it from a phone company), continues to be very easy. Just grab the phone and swipe up from underneath the screen.

What goes on next depends upon your security configurations. Unless you have a passcode, you'll go to the Home screen. If you do have a passcode, Face ID may recognize that person and take you to the home screen. Or, if you have a passcode but avoid Face ID, you will have to enter your code. Regardless of your configurations, unlocking requires a simple swipe.

How to Go back to the Home Screen on iPhone X

Having a physical Home button, time for the home screen from any application just required pushing a button. Even without that button, though, time for the

Home screen is fairly simple.

Just swipe up an extremely brief distance from underneath of the screen. An extended swipe does another thing (check another item to get more on that), but an instant little flick will need you out of any application and back to the Home screen.

How to Open up the iPhone X Multitasking View

On previous iPhones, double-clicking the home button raised a multitasking view that enables you to see all open up apps, quickly change to new apps, and easily quit applications that are working.

That same view continues to be on the iPhone X; nevertheless, you get access to it differently. Swipe up from underneath in regards to a third of just how up the screen. This is just a little hard initially because it's like the shorter swipe that goes to the home screen.

Switching Apps Without Starting Multitasking on iPhone X

Here's an example in which eliminating the home button presents a completely new feature; it doesn't can be found on other models. Rather than having to open up the multitasking view from the last item to improve apps, you can change to a fresh app with only a simple swipe.

At the bottom corners of the screen, about a level with the line at the bottom, swipe still left or right. Doing that will leap you into the next or earlier application from the multitasking view-a considerably faster way to go.

Using Reachability on iPhone X

With ever-bigger screens on iPhones, it could be hard to attain things that are definately not your thumb. The Reachability feature that was first launched on the iPhone 6 series solves that. An instant double-touch of the home button brings the very best of the screen down, so it is simpler to reach.

Around the iPhone X, Reachability continues to be a choice, though it's disabled by default (transform it on by going to *Settings* -> *General* -> *Accessibility* -> *Reachability*). Whether it's on, you can gain access to the feature by swiping down on the screen near the collection in the bottom. That may be just a little hard to understand, and that means you can also swipe along rapidly from the same location.

New Methods to Do Old Jobs: Siri, Apple Pay, and More

You will find loads of other common iPhone features that use the home button. Here's how to execute some of the most typical ones on the iPhone X:

- ***Take Screenshots***: Click on the Side and volume up buttons at exactly the same time.
- ***Change Off/Restart***: Press and contain the Part and volume up buttons at exactly the same time.
- ***Activate Siri***: Press and contain the Side button.
- ***Confirm Apple Pay and iTunes/App Store Buys***: Use Face ID.

Where is Control Center?

If you know your iPhone, you might be wondering about Control Center. This useful group of tools and shortcuts is utilized by swiping up from underneath the screen on other models. Since swiping around underneath of the screen does so a great many other things on the iPhone X, Control Center is elsewhere upon this model.

To gain access to it, swipe down from the very best right part of the screen (to the right of the notch), and Control Center appears. Touch or swipe the screen again to dismiss it if you are done.

Want a Home Button? Add One Using Software

Wish your iPhone X had a Home button? Well, you can't

get a hardware button, but there's a way to get one using the software. The AssistiveTouch feature adds an on-screen Home button for individuals with physical conditions that prevent them from easily clicking the home button (or for people that have broken Home buttons). Anyone can change it and use that same software/virtual button.

To allow AssistiveTouch:

- Touch *Settings*.
- Touch *General*.
- Touch *Accessibility*.
- Touch *AssistiveTouch.*
- Move the AssistiveTouch slider to On/green, and a button shows up on the screen that is capable of doing some of the home button's tasks.

Chapter 11

iPhone X Face ID Hidden Features

Reduce Alarm Volume and Keep Screen Brightness with Attention Awareness

Because Face ID can show when you're taking a look at your iPhone's screen, it can make your iPhone respond with techniques that produce sense predicated on your attention. You need to ensure that the interest Aware Features option is geared up by pursuing these steps:

- Tap Settings.
- Tap Face ID & Passcode.
- Get into your passcode.
- Move the interest Aware Features slider to

ON/Green

When you do this:

- ***When you have an alarm going off***: and also you go through the screen, the volume of the alarm will automatically lower because the telephone knows it got your attention.

- ***The screen won't dim to save lots of battery***: Normally, the screen automatically dims after a brief period, if the telephone sees you are looking at the screen, it understands you're utilizing it and that you would like to start to see the screen.

Get Notification Previews Without Notification Center

Normally, viewing full previews of notifications delivered to you by applications requires starting

Notification Center. Not with Face ID. Since Face ID identifies you and unlocks your mobile phone, there is no risk that another person is viewing your private content. Due to that, changing your notification configurations can provide you with full notification previews without starting Notification Center. Here's how:

- Tap *Settings*.
- Touch *Notifications*.
- Touch *Show Previews*.
- Touch When Unlocked

Now, when you get a notification on your lock screen, take a look at your telephone (but don't swipe through to the screen to unlock it). When Face ID identifies you, the notification will raise to show the entire preview.

Autofill Passwords in Safari

The Autofill is your password as it pertains to authorizing payments or unlocking your phone with Face ID. Do you realize you can also utilize it to log into websites in Safari on the iPhone X?

That is right: if you store your usernames and passwords in Safari to be auto-filled when you come to login screens, Face ID keeps your that data secure, and functional only by you. Some tips about what you must do:

- *Save website usernames and passwords in Safari when you log in to the sites by touchping the pop-up menu.*
- *Enable Face ID* to autofill those usernames and

passwords by going to Settings -> Face ID & Passcode -> enter your passcode -> moving the Safari Autofill slider to On/Green.

- Visit a website where you have a merchant account preserved in Safari and go directly to the login screen.

- Touch the username or password field.

- Above the Safari keyboard, touch Passwords.

- In the menu that arises from underneath, touch an individual account you want to use.

- When the facial ID icon appears on the screen, position your iPhone X to scan that person. When Face ID authenticates you, your security password is added.

- Log in to the website.

Control Which Apps Can Gain access to Face ID

Every app that would require that you to sign in would want to use Face ID since it's faster and better. Your real face scans aren't distributed to the applications (Apple converts the facial scan into an *abstract code*, so there is no risk that any applications could steal that info), nevertheless, you might not want every application to have that access to (you can control how many other data applications can gain access too). If not, here's how to regulate which apps gain access to Face ID:

- Tap *Settings*.
- Touch *Face ID & Passcode*.
- Get into your passcode.

- Tap Other Apps

This screen lists all the applications installed on your iPhone that are looking to use Face ID. To stop apps from being able to access it, move the slider next to these to Off/white.

Switch OFF Face ID Quickly with Buttons

If you're in times where you come to mind that you may be required to use Face ID to unlock your mobile phone and reveal your data-for instance, during a conversation with the authorities or when crossing country borders-you may choose to switch off Face ID. And if time is vital in these circumstances, you will want to do it fast. Listed below are two ways to carefully turn off Face ID by pressing control keys on the iPhone X:

- At exactly the same time, press and contain the side button on the right of the telephone and either volume button (or both, if you like. Either works); this goes to the Shut down/Emergency screen. Face ID is currently off and also to unlock the telephone; you will be prompted to enter your passcode.

- Press the medial side button five times in quick succession; this causes the Emergency SOS feature, which brings extremely loud siren audio with it, so be ready for that. Touch Cancel on the Emergency SOS screen and then touch Stop Calling to get rid of the decision and the siren. Face ID is currently off.

Use Siri to Turn Off Face ID carefully

In addition to all or any the other activities Siri can do, additionally, it may switch off Face ID for you. That is helpful for quickly turning off Face ID in the situations described earlier. You must have *"Hey Siri"* allowed for this feature to work, but if you need to do, here's what you must do:

- Without unlocking your telephone, tell it, "Hey Siri, whose telephone is this?"
- Siri will screen whatever info they have about you-generally a name, picture, plus some contact information (unless you want to buy even to show this, remove that from the Address Publication). At exactly the same time, Face ID has been disabled.

- Now, to unlock the telephone or to change Face ID on-again, enter your passcode.

Make Face ID Unlock Faster

Feel just like Face ID takes too much time to identify you and unlock your iPhone? You can speed up the procedure by tweaking:

- Touch *Settings*.
- Touch *Face ID & Passcode*.
- Insert your password.
- Move the *Require Attention for Face ID* slider to Off/white

This boosts *Face ID* speed, but it additionally makes your phone less secure. The *Require Attention* ensures that you are looking at the iPhone and also have your eyes open up for Face ID to unlock your mobile phone. By turning it off, things go faster; however, your telephone could be unlocked even if you are asleep, unconscious, or attempting not to adhere to someone wanting to pressure you to unlock your mobile phone. Keep that risk at heart as you select whether to improve the settings.

Improve Face ID Accuracy

If Face ID doesn't recognize you and the passcode screen appears, enter your passcode immediately; when you do this, Face ID requires the checking of that person it didn't authorize. Adding the new check to the initial, it identifies that person from more perspectives and in more situations.

Face ID eventually throws these short-term matches out because they're not the area of the original, authoritative checkout. But, for some time, they help Face ID work a little much better.

If Face ID often does not identify you correctly, you almost certainly want to create it up again with a fresh face check by going through the process: *Configurations -> Face ID & Passcode -> enter your passcode -> Reset Face ID and then manage it again.*

Chapter 12

All iPhone X Series Gestures to Know

Touch to Wake iPhone X

You may get glanceable information from your iPhone and never have to unlock it. Touch the screen to wake your lock screen; this interaction pays if you would like to check the time, look into your notifications, or check battery level while your iPhone is charging. From here, you can also quickly start the Torch feature or activate the Camera.

Lift to Wake iPhone X

Much like touch to wake, lifting your phone provides you glanceable information and never have to do other things.

You additionally have speedy usage of the Torch and Camera, but because of the iPhone's position, the TrueDepth camera system likely has a definite view of that person, letting you unlock it with a straightforward swipe up from underneath of the screen.

Unlock iPhone X

Among the key top features of the iPhone X lineup is Face ID. To unlock your device, make sure the True Depth camera (homed within the notch near the top of the screen) has a distinct view of that person. Then, swipe up from underneath the screen.

If you are wearing dark sunglasses or that person is otherwise obscured, Face ID won't work correctly. Instead, you'll be asked to enter your device pin.

Return to the Home Screen

Using the omission of the physical home button, it isn't necessarily apparent how to come back to the home screen. However, all you have to do is swipe up from the home bar situated in the bottom of the screen to consider you back again to the main screen.

Gain access to and Manage Notifications on iPhone X

To visit a set of your notifications, swipe down from the left part of the screen notch (the medial side showing time). You will see your notifications (if you have any) grouped by app.

- To do this about the same notification, touch it to

release that app.

- With grouped notifications, touch to expand, then touch the notification you want to start.
- To control a notification, swipe it still left to reveal additional management options.
- To clear all notifications, touch X, and then touch Clear.

Access Control Center on iPhone X

To gain access to Control Center, swipe down from the right of the notch (the medial side showing the network indicator and electric battery level). This step would provide you with fast access to settings such as Wi-Fi, Bluetooth, Volume, and more.

You can even access Control Center from the lock screen using the same gesture. Just ensure that your screen is awake.

Adjust Settings in charge Center on iPhone X

Once in charge Center, you can easily adjust specific configurations using 3D Touch (iPhone X, XS, XS Max) or long-press (iPhone XR).

For example, if you would like to improve the screen brightness, press down (or press and keep) showing the settings pub. From here, you can swipe up or right down to adjust the lighting. Additionally, these windows provide quick options for activating Nighttime adjustment setting and True Firmness.

Quickly Change Between Apps on iPhone X

To go between an application, you're currently using and recently used ones, swipe directly on the home bar in the bottom of the screen. This step lets you slip along to the application you were utilizing prior.

You would keep swiping to scroll through the newest applications in their order of last use. To return to the prior app, swipe left on the home bar. This step is advantageous when you need to move back-and-forth frequently between two apps.

Change Between Apps on iPhone X

To obtain a fuller view of your lately used apps, swipe up from your home bar, stopping halfway in the screen and then moving your finger somewhat to the right. This step would reveal a purchased carousel of lately used apps. From here, you can swipe through them and touch the main one you want to open up.

Turn OFF Apps on iPhone X

If you want to close an application that's misbehaving, you can do so by uncovering the full application switcher. From here, swipe through to the application you want to turn off to eliminate it from the carousel, therefore shutting it down completely.

Activate Reachability on iPhone X

If you've ever found it hard to attain the very best of your iPhone screen, Reachability is a good tool to glide the screen area down. To get this done, swipe down on the dock in the bottom of the screen. Features at the very top would now become more accessible.

To come back to the typical view, swipe down over the home pub or press the tiny carat near the top of the screen area.

<u>Access Today View on iPhone X</u>

To gain access to Today View, swipe from the first web page of your home screen. This step would reveal your selection of app widgets. To return to the home screen, swipe right or up from underneath of the screen.

Access Siri Search iPhone X

Siri Search pays if you would like to find across your device and apps. To get this done, make sure you're on the home screen, then swipe down from the centre of the screen. This move would release a search feature near the top of the screen and talk about your keyboard.

Chapter 13

How to Use iPhones without Home Button: X, XS, & XR

Gestures on the iPhone’s touchscreen will always be important, but without the Home button the iPhone X and later models, gestures become essential. To execute functions just like a turn off or time for the Home screen on your iPhone X, XS, XS Max, or XR, you are going to use unique gestures that combine the medial side and Volume control keys instead of the lacking Home button. Common features, like speaking with Siri, starting Apple Pay, and shutting apps, will have unique gestures that utilize your phone's physical control keys, Face ID, and the touchscreen. This chapter addresses all the tips you should know, like how to use Reachability, have a screenshot, as well as how to briefly disable Face ID the iPhone X, XS, XS Max, and XR. Let’s get started doing how to use gestures to get around iPhone models X and later.

There are a great number of new gestures and changes to navigate the iPhone, given that Apple did away with the Home button. You're probably acquainted with the most common iPhone gestures, such as pinching with two fingertips to focus or Tremble to Undo. You can also pull multiple photos and drop them into another app. Gestures on the iPhone will always be an integral part of routine, however the iPhone X launched a lot of new ways to do old stuff. Unless in any other case indicated, these procedures all connect with the iPhone X, XS, XS MAX, and XR.

How to Unlock Your iPhone with Raise to Wake

Raise to Wake is fired up by default on the iPhone X and other newer models. To use *Raise to Wake* on the iPhone X, XS, XS Max, or XR, lift your iPhone, and the screen will automatically start. If *Raise to Wake* isn't working, likely, you have accidentally handicapped the feature inside Configurations.

How to Enable Raise to Wake:

- Open up the Settings app.
- Select Screen & Brightness.
- Toggle Raise to Wake to the ON position to allow the feature.

You don't need to lift your phone awaken the screen on iPhone X; you can merely touch the screen to awaken your iPhone X, even if Raise to Wake is impaired.

How to Go back to the Home screen From an App

Returning to the home screen can appear impossible if there is no Home button. Around the iPhone X, XS, XS Max, and XR, you can go back to your Home screen by following the instructios below.

How to Go back to the Home Screen:

- From within any app, place your finger on the home bar underneath the center of the screen.
- Swipe up toward the very top of your screen.

How to Unlock the iPhone X & Newer iPhones

To unlock your iPhone X, XS, XS Max, or XR, you will need to ensure that a Face ID is established. Using Face ID, you can boost or tap your iPhone X, or other newer models, to wake and unlock your iPhone by looking straight at the screen.

How exactly to Unlock an iPhone X or Later Using Face ID:

- Wake the screen up by either tapping the screen or using Raise to Wake.
- Look directly at the screen to use Face ID to unlock your device.
- Swipe up from underneath of your Lock screen to visit the Home screen.

- If, for just about any reason, Face ID didn't unlock your mobile phone, swipe up from underneath of the screen to retry Face ID or even to enter your passcode instead. Once you have input your passcode, your iPhone will automatically go back to the Home screen, or whatever application was open up last.

How to Open up the Control & Notification Centers

The notch on the iPhone X and later models divide the very best of the screen into a left and right hands screen. On your own iPhone X, XR, XS, or XS MAX, the right part of the notch near the top of the screen is used to gain access to your Control Center while the left side is utilized to open up Notifications.

- To open Control Center, swipe down from the right hand side of the screen.
- To open Notifications, swipe down from the left hand side of the screen.

How to Gain access to Siri with the medial side Button

Removing the home button also changes how you access Siri on the iPhone X and newer models.

- If you wish to use gestures rather than Hey Siri on the iPhone X, XS, XS Max, or XR, then you will have to use the medial side button to gain access to Siri.

- Click and hold the side button (formerly known as the Rest/Wake button) to speak to Siri.

How exactly to Activate Apple Pay

On previous iPhone models, twice tapping the home button raised Apple Pay from a locked screen, but on the iPhone X or later you will have to use a fresh gesture to gain access to **Apple Pay**. To use Apple Pay from a locked screen on the iPhone X, XS, XS Max, or XR, you will have to double click your side button and use Face ID to continue with Apple Pay. Here's how to use Apple Pay on iPhones without a Home button:

- Double click on the Part button to open up Apple Pay

- Look into your iPhone screen to verify with Face

ID.

If Apple Pay doesn't appear when the medial side button is double-clicked, 1 of 2 things is undoubtedly going on: either you haven't created a debit card with Apple Pay (check even though you have; my cards disappeared after establishing my new iPhone) or you do not have Apple Pay allowed in settings; this is fixed with the next steps:

- Open up the Settings app.
- Select Face ID & Passcode.
- Toggle ON **Apple Pay** under Use **Face ID** For.

How to Take Screenshots without the home Button

Sometimes, you will need to have a screenshot to save lots of an important formula as a graphic or to keep hold of a text to examine later.

- To have a screen shot on the iPhone X, XS, XS Max, or XR, you'll use a mixture of the medial side and volume buttons rather than utilizing a Home button.

- To consider screenshot on your iPhone X, or a later model iPhone, concurrently press and release the medial side button and Volume Up button.

How to Enable & Activate Reachability

Reachability slashes off the low fifty percent of the screen and moves the very best part of your screen to underneath, making it simpler to reach the very best of your screen with one hand. By default, Reachability has switched off on the X, XS, XS Max, and XR; nevertheless, you can allow the Reachability feature inside the Settings portion of your Configurations app.

To allow Reachability on your iPhone X, XS, XS MAX, or XR:

- Open up the Settings app.
- Select General.
- Touch Accessibility.
- Toggle on Reachability.

- Swipe down on the home bar or bottom level middle of the screen to activate Reachability.

Given that you've allowed Reachability, you can activate the feature within any application by swiping down on the horizontal part, also called the home feature, at the bottom of your screen. There is no home pub on the home screen, nevertheless, you can still activate Reachibility on the home screen by swiping down from underneath middle of the screen where you'll normally find the home feature.

How to Change Between & Force Quit Apps

You will find two various ways to change between applications on the iPhone X: with the App Switcher and without. You can gain access to the App Switcher on the iPhone X, XS, XS Max, and XR by partly swiping upwards from underneath the screen. You can even switch between applications by swiping the home bar still left or right.

How to Open up the App Switcher on the iPhone X, XS, XS Max, or XR:

- Swipe halfway up from underneath the screen.
- Lift your finger, and the App Switcher will open up. You can swipe through, much like previous models, and touch on an application to open up it.
- To eliminate an application from App Switcher, swipe through to the app.

To switch applications without starting the App Switcher:

- Place your finger on the home bar or underneath the middle of the screen if the home button is absent.

- Swipe from left to open up your latest applications in descending order.

How to Temporarily Disable Face ID

Face ID is not a perfect system; users have reported that some family members have had the opportunity to use cell phones protected Face ID due to a solid family resemblance. To briefly disable Face ID, you will have to keep down the medial side and Volume Up control keys to talk about the turn off screen, and then tap Cancel to Force your iPhone to require the passcode to unlock briefly.

Here's how to briefly disable ***Face ID*** on the iPhone X, XS, XS Max, or XR:

- Hold down the Volume Up or Down button and

the medial side button simultaneously.

- After the shutdown screen appears, forget about the buttons. That is important; if you keep up to carry down the control keys, Emergency SOS will automatically be brought on.

- Touch the X at the bottom to cancel the shutdown.

Now, Face ID is briefly handicapped until you enter your passcode. Once you enter your passcode, Face ID will continue working as typical.

How to Switch OFF Power & Perform a hard Restart

The Home button was central to numerous functions, including powering down your iPhone or forcing a hard restart whenever your iPhone freeze. To power down or push a hard restart on the iPhone X, XS, XS MAX, and XR, you will have to perform new gestures that involve a mixture of the medial side and Volume Up buttons.

To turn from the iPhone X, XS, XS Max, or XR:

- Hold down the medial side button and Volume Up or Down button before option to slip to power off shows up.

- Using the Slip to Force Off toggle, swipe to the right.

You can even switch off the iPhone X, XS, XS Max, or XR from the overall portion of the Settings app.

- Open up the Settings application and choose *General*.

- scroll completely down to underneath, and tap

TURN OFF.

- Glide to power icon to turn the power off.

You are capable of doing a hard restart, sometimes called a force shutdown, on your iPhone X, XS, XS Max, or XR. To execute a hard restart:

- Quickly press and release the Volume Up accompanied by the Volume Down button.

- Now, press and maintain the side button before device shuts down, and the Apple logo design appears.

- Your iPhone will automatically restart.

It’s good to notice that whenever performing a hard Restart, it requires the iPhone X a couple of seconds to turn off when you’re pressing the medial side button. So don’t quit! I thought it wasn't working initially, but I needed to sustain the side button pressed down for a longer length of time.

How to Power Off the iPhone X & Newer Models

Sometimes, you will need to power your iPhone off for a movie, a lecture, or other events that want your full attention. Like previous models, whenever your iPhone X, XS, XS Max, or XR are run off, then you will have to use a gesture to turn your iPhone back On carefully.

To carefully *Turn On* the iPhone X or later models, press and maintain the side button before the Apple logo design appears.

Chapter 14

Steps to Make Folders & Group Apps on the iPhone

Creating folders on your iPhone is a sensible way to reduce mess on your home screen. Grouping apps collectively can also make it simpler to use your phone - if all your music applications are in the same place, you will not have to be searching through folders or looking at your mobile phone when you wish to utilize them.

How you create folders isn't immediately obvious, but once you understand the secret, it's simple — some tips about what you should know about how to make a folder on your iPhone.

How to Create Folders and Group Apps on the iPhone

- To make a folder, you will need at least two applications to place into the folder. Determine which two you want to use.

- Gently touch and hold one of the applications until all applications on the screen start shaking (this is the same process that you utilize to re-arrange apps).

  NOTE: Making folders on the iPhone 6S and 7 series, the iPhone 8 and iPhone X, and iPhone XS and XR, is just a little trickier. That's because the 3D Touchscreen on those models responds differently to different presses on the screen. When you have one particular cell phones, don't press too much or you'll result in a menu or shortcut. Only a light touch and hold will do.

- Pull one of the applications at the top the other. When the first application appears to merge into the second one, take your finger from the screen. Dropping one form into the other creates the folder.
- What goes on next depends upon what version of the iOS you're working with or using.
  - In iOS 7 and higher, the folder and its own recommended name take up the whole screen.
  - In iOS 4-6, you Typically the two applications and a name for the folder in a strip over the screen
- Every folder has a name assigned to it by default (more on this in a moment); nevertheless, you can transform that name by touching the x icon to clear

the recommended name and then type the name you want.

- If you wish to add more applications to the folder, touch the wallpaper to close the folder. Then pull more apps into the new folder.

- When you've added all the applications you want and edited the name, click on the Home button on the leading Center of the iPhone as well as your changes will be saved (precisely like when re-arranging icons).

TIPS: *When you have an iPhone X, XS, XR, or newer, there is no Home button to click. Instead, you should tap* ***Done*** *at the right part of the screen.*

How Default iPhone Folder Titles Are Suggested

When you initially create a folder, the iPhone assigns a suggested name to it. That name is chosen predicated on the App Store category that the applications in the folder result from; for instance, if the applications result from the Video games category, the recommended name of the folder is Video games. You should use the recommended name or add your own using the instructions in steps above.

How to Edit Folders on Your iPhone

If you have already created a folder on your iPhone, you might edit it by changing the name, adding or removing apps, and more. Here's how:

- To edit a pre-existing folder, touch and contain the folder until it starts to move.
- Touch it another time, and the folder will open up, and its material will fill up the screen.
- You may make the next changes
  - Edit the folder's name by tapping on the written text.
  - Add more applications by dragging them in.
  - Remove applications from the folder by dragging them away.
- Click on the Home button or the Done button to save lots of your changes.

How to Remove Apps From Folders on iPhone

If you wish to remove an application from a folder on your iPhone or iPod touch, follow these steps:

- Touch and contain the folder that you would like to eliminate the application from.
- When the applications and folders start wiggling, remove your finger from the screen.
- Touch the folder you want to eliminate the application from.
- Drag the application from the folder and onto the home screen.
- Click on the Home or Done button to save lots of the new set up.

How to Add Folders to the iPhone Dock

The four applications over the bottom of the iPhone reside in what's called the Dock. You can include folders to the dock if you'd like. To achieve that:

- Move one of the applications currently in the dock away by tapping, keeping, and dragging it to the primary section of the home screen.
- Move a folder into the space.
- Press the home or Done button, depending on your iPhone model, to save lots of the change.

How to Delete a Folder on the iPhone

Deleting a folder is comparable to eliminating an app. Some tips about what you must do:

- Pull all the applications from the folder and onto the home screen.
- When you do that, the folder disappears.
- Press the home or Done button to save lots of the change, and you're done.

Chapter 15

Useful iPhone XR & XS Tricks & Tips

You need to Know

Control Your Apple TV With iPhone XR & XS

The Control Focus on the iPhone XR & XS has an awesome trick: it enables you to regulate your Apple TV if you have one. So long as your iPhone XR or XS and Apple Television are on a single cellular network, it'll work. Get into Control Center and then look for the Apple Television button that shows up. Touch it and start managing your Apple Television.

How to Calm iPhone Xr & Xs Alarms with Your Face

An extremely cool feature of the iPhone XR & XS is

Face ID. It gives you to unlock your phone just by taking a look at it. Face ID also has various other cool features-like that one. Whenever your iPhone XR or XS security alarm goes off, you can silent it by just picking right up your iPhone and taking a look at it; this tells your iPhone you understand about the arm, and it'll quiet it.

How to Enable USB Limited Setting on iPhone XR & XS

Apple just built a robust new security feature into the iPhone XR & XS with the latest version of iOS; this launch is what's known as ***USB Limited Setting*** to the iPhone XR & XS. Lately, companies have been making devices that may be connected to an iPhone's USB slot and crack an iPhone's passcode.

To protect from this, Apple has introduced a USB Restricted Setting. USB Restricted Setting disabled data writing between an iPhone and a USB device if the iPhone is not unlocked to get more than one hour; this effectively makes the iPhone breaking boxes ineffective as they may take hours or times to unlock a locked iPhone.

By default, ***USB Limited Mode*** is enabled in iOS. But for those who want to disable it, or make sure it hasn't been disabled, go to the *Configurations app* and touch *Face ID & Passcode*. Enter your passcode and then swipe down until you visit a section entitled ***"Allow Access When Locked."***

The final toggle in this section is a field that says *"USB Accessories."* The toggle next to them should be turned OFF (white); this implies *USB Restricted Setting* is allowed, and devices can't download or upload data from/to your iPhone if the iPhone is not unlocked to get more than one hour.

How decelerate the two times click necessary for Apple Pay

Given that the iPhone XR & XS jettisoned the Touch ID sensor, you confirm your ***Apple Pay*** obligations by using Face ID and twice pressing the medial side button. By default, you will need to dual press the medial side button pretty quickly-but it is possible to make things slow down.

To take action, go to *Settings* > *General* > *Availability*. Now scroll right down to Side Button. Privately Button screen, you can select between *default, gradual, or slowest*. Pick the speed that is most effective for you.

Quickly Disable Face ID

Depending on your geographical area, the police might be able to legally demand you uncover your smartphone at that moment via its facial recognition features. For reasons unknown, facial biometrics aren't protected in the manner fingerprints, and passcodes are; in a few localities. That's why Apple has generated an attribute that lets you quickly disable Face ID in a pinch without going into your settings. Just press the side button five times, and Face ID will be disabled, and you'll need to enter your passcode instead to gain access to your phone.

Use Two Pane Scenery View

This tip only pertains to the iPhone XS Max but is cool nonetheless. If you keep your XS device horizontally when using specific applications you'll see lots of the built-in apps changes to a two-pane setting, including Email and Records. This setting is the main one you observe on an iPad where, for example, you can see a list of all of your records in the Records app while positively reading or editing a solitary note.

Chapter 16

5 Ways of Upgrading Your iPhone Digital Photography for Instagram

1. **Minimalism is Key**

Our number 1 Instagram photography suggestion is to consider photos that look great and professional with your iPhone; you would need to believe. Why? Because it is not only better - but it's much simpler to choose one exciting subject matter and make that the center point of your image.

The sure sign of the amateur is a person who tries to match so many subjects to their imagery. "But my image would be filled with vacant space!" you may protest. That's flawlessly fine. Professional photographers call bare space, *'negative space'*, which is another technique which makes your center point stand out.

The ultimate way to do this is to go closer to the topic and remove anything in the shot that may distract the viewer.

This can make your Instagram photography appear to be like it was done by an expert. As you keep up to apply this, you'll come to find that minimalism is the most shared on systems like Instagram, because photos with ONE center point stick out on smartphone screens.

2. **Get low in Position**

Understandably, your camera move shouldn't be filled with selfies. Just as your camera move shouldn't contain images used at chest elevation.

Among the quickest ways to update your Instagram digital photography and create images that stick out is to take from a lesser position than what you're used to. You don't need to get too low either, capture from less than what you're used to.

When you take your subject or centre point from such a minimal angle that the sky is the only background, what you finish up doing is following both Instagram picture taking Tip 1 and Tip 2 - making the image extremely attractive on the system like Instagram.

So when you're finally more comfortable with the thought of looking, "extra" according to some people, you'll be able to start squatting and even kneeling to be able to get the best low-angle images.

3. Depth of Field

Exactly what does *"depth of field"* mean? Blurring backgrounds, of course! Everyone knows an image with blur looks a lot more interesting than a graphic where the background and the foreground are both in concentration.

When you utilize zoom lens accessories to mention a feeling of depth in your images, i.e. Telephoto lenses, you'll be able to attract people's attention - whether you're photographing accessories for Instagram, or just taking a scenery photograph.

Besides getting hold of iPhone accessories, a straightforward technique like using "leading lines" that direct the audiences' focus on whatever it is that has been photographed is a superb way to produce depth for your Instagram digital photography. For instance, going for a picture of the road, railway track, a riverbank, fences, and pathways are an excellent leading line!

Once you have found your leads, you can create some depth in the foreground by using found items like stones or leaves or other things, for example, When you absolutely cannot find anything in the foreground that could add a component appealing, then get back to Suggestion #2 and "Get Low in position"! Take from a lesser angle, and you will be amazed what you can catch.

4. **Get Up-Close and Personal**

Okay, so right now, you've probably determined that each of the tips accumulates from the prior tips so that by enough time you've mastered this whole list, you're practically an expert!

Your Instagram picture taking needs details! It might be hard to trust, but a great deal of iPhone professional photographers make the error of not getting close enough to the centre point. Particularly when they're photographing something with a great deal of fine detail - i.e. When you capture from a long distance, the picture eventually ends up being a little dull and impersonal; however, when you get near to the thing, you all of a sudden have an image that involves life - particularly when you take portraits of others or even your selfies. When you move nearer to the subject, you can properly catch cosmetic features and feelings that would build relationships with the viewer.

Even the newer iPhones remain unable to shoot HQ images of subject matter close up and personal, so our reward Instagram photography suggestion is that you would have to get your hands on the macro zoom lens, like the ***TrueLux macro zoom lens***.

What this zoom lens can do is allow your camera to target incredibly near to whatever you're shooting and then add visual interest (and depth) to your photograph, simultaneously.

5. Don't Be Scared of the Silhouette

That one seems just like a no-brainer, but many individuals continue to be afraid to embrace silhouettes on the Instagram grid.

First of all, ***what is a silhouette?*** *It's mostly when an object's form is captured against a gleaming light. It's not the same thing as a shadow.*

Silhouettes add an air of secret to an image, and against

an extremely bright background, a silhouette really can look quite beautiful on your Instagram feed!

Another best part concerning this particular Instagram photography technique is that it is really simple to create images of a silhouette on your iPhone. You just need to know what you want to take a picture of, and then capture towards the light. That's it!

If you'd like to ensure that your subject's silhouette looks unmistakable but still dark, check out your iPhone camera app, tap the screen to create the focus, and then swipe right down to darken the camera exposure - you can still darken the subject even further with photography editing apps.

The optimum time to consider silhouette photographs, despite having your iPhone, is during what professional photographers refer to as the *golden hours of sunrise and sunset.* When sunlight is low coming, then you can position the source of light behind the topic, which means that you'll get a perfectly coloured sky as the backdrop - taking benefit of tips 1 to 4.

You do not necessarily have to hold back for the golden hour to consider silhouette photographs, so long as your source of light is behind the subject.

For instance, if you are shooting indoors, you merely have to put your subject before the window (to consider advantage of daylight), or before a band light/ softbox if daylight is no option.